AN ADVENTURER'S GUIDE TO THE NEXT AGE

AN ADVENTURER'S GUIDE TO THE NEXT AGE

By Kriston Couchey

This book is dedicated to my mother, Louise Maccarone, whose prayers and love have kept and shaped me for such a time as this. And, to Ron McGatlin who has had the grace and foresight of a spiritual father to see that Father has placed within me the Word of the Kingdom, even in a flawed earthen vessel. I also want to thank David Reynolds for His labor of love in editing and adapting text to help it make sense.

Introduction

This book is the result of an ongoing verbal interaction with Father and flowed as a 'parabolic understanding' from successive encounters. The first part is a record of four experiential engagements with the Godhead and my personal witness to this Truth as received from Father.

The remaining writings, not in parables, are words of prophecy and wisdom. They form a foundational context for His sons and daughters to engage in, to continue the maturity journey that is in Father's heart for us all. I pray as you read these words you are encouraged and challenged. I also pray you will discern the difference between what Father is saying and what is of man.

PART ONE

THE MOUNTAIN OF ASCENSION

CHAPTER ONE

THE MOUNTAIN AND THE CITY

Dangling from the edge of the cliff, I struggled once again to pull myself up onto the level plain before me which capped the top of the mountain. At least a hundred times in the last 10 years I had come to this same place of clear vision, only to lose my grip and fall back down with bumps and bruises to a ledge far below the cloud line, dazed and confused.

This time however, as I inevitably began to slip, a voice rang out to me, "Do you trust me?" It was Him! He appeared in brightness before me with an outstretched arm. I now knew in my heart why I had fallen so often. I was overwhelmed by fear! Fear of losing my own life. The same fear the Israelites in the desert felt when the clouds and smoke covered the holy mountain, and they ran because they feared to die before the Face of God. This fear was really unbelief in Father's ability to take care of me if I chose to let go of everything, even my own life!

I then realized that letting go of my own life had been His goal all along and that the struggle to save my life must end now. Fear did not leave, but I made my decision and like a little child I reached out to grasp His outstretched hand and surrendered to the unknown. Trembling I extended my hand and said, "Yes, I trust you..."

I wept as His presence surrounded me and I was swept up into His arms of love. Fear vanished in an instant and what overtook me was glorious Peace. I no longer had any need to worry, I was standing in a broad place with His love and peace overshadowing me and I was safe. But more importantly I KNEW, more deeply than I had even known before, that He was my God!

He had told me years ago that He would be my God and now I knew that He truly was. He said, "It's not that you tried, it's that you died! Through trying and finding only failure, you found the very end of yourself, but trying was never going to get you onto this level plain."

A WITNESS

It was my everlasting Father who held me dear and spoke tenderly to me. I was wrapped in His abiding presence that drove out all my fears and blanketed me with peace. I had been here before, but only as a revelatory experience to help me press on to seek out this place with Him. I began to realize that what I had seen and experienced as divine revelation in the Spirit had now become a reality.

"You have been a witness to the truth", He said. "Up till now you have been given revelation as a witness to others of the Truth I have been speaking to them. By the mouth of two or three is something established; my Spirit, and the revelation given to my countless witnesses, have helped establish my kingdom in the hearts of many of my children who have been seeking me. But, the day of simply being a witness of revelation alone is coming to an end and the day of the manifestation of that revelation is beginning."

The brightness of His glory kept me from seeing His form clearly, but I could now see His eyes; eyes of Love that were swirls of fire. I then asked the question, "But, what about those witnesses who have not made it here yet? What will become of them?" He replied, "There are still more that will overcome and meet Me here. But, at this time, many of my witnesses have themselves been overcome."

BABYLON

He then stretched out his hand and pointed to the plains below the mountain. "Behold Babylon!" - He said.

As far as my eyes could see on the plain below, there was a mass of humanity as vast as the ocean; a churning, moving, crashing sea of humanity, milling together in deep confusion. In the midst of this sea of humanity was a large city set upon seven hills. I realized that much of the motion was from the movement of people and beasts bearing burdens in and out of the city. They were bearing these burdens back and forth from the four corners of the plain which seemed to have no end.

The city itself was sprawling and it was hard to see where it began and ended. It was built as a mass of confusion with no regular pattern to its towers and buildings. Yet all its structures were made of worthless material; shards of broken wood, hay and stubble, it reminded me of Paul's words in Corinthians about the materials men build with. As I looked more closely, I saw that the burdens carried by both beasts of burden and men were made of the same worthless materials, yet the men were hoarding and trading these 'treasures' as if they were precious.

My eyes then followed a trail of traders to the base of the mountain upon which I stood. To my shock I saw that much of the mountainside was covered with small enclaves of buildings made of the same worthless materials. Most of these people were milling about the structures below the level of the clouds, yet I could see through these clouds without difficulty. A few who had traveled above the clouds were busy climbing. The numbers of people on the mountain were not as numerous as those on the plain, but the trading of the goods of Babylon back and forth among the separate enclaves had the same look of confusion that dominated the masses on the plain.

"Who are they?" I asked, pointing to those settling and building on the mountain. He replied, "Some of these people are journeying their way to the top of the mountain as you have already done. Many others have chosen to build and settle on the mountainside and have been overcome by the lure of Babylon."

In horror I began to recognize some of the people and places that I had met on my journey that I had once tried to become part of and left in dissatisfaction. During the time of my travels, these places had seemed so elegant and alluring. But from the top of the Mountain their appearance was that of disheveled and appalling shanty towns, fashioned together with wood, hay and stubble.

Father continued, "These places were built by those who had been given my gifts and revelation to help men come to the top of my Mountain. Many of them had a clear revelation of the top of the mountain and gathered men unto themselves to share that revelation. However, they have built their shanty towns of wood, hay and stubble around the very revelation and gifts they were given to bring my people here."

I then noticed some of the enclaves had signs that read 'The New Jerusalem'. He continued speaking, "Many of these leaders have had a revelatory vision of the New Jerusalem but have settled for the praise of men and have believed the delusion that they actually are building the Holy City."

I noticed that some dissatisfied people were leaving the larger enclaves and beginning to make the trek up the mountain. Others, who had also recognized the bankrupt state of the shanty towns, began to gather themselves in smaller groups and began building their own disheveled shanties apart from everyone else.

To my amazement and horror, I saw them begin to build almost exact replicas of the places they had just left, only smaller. Everything built by man on the mountainside was simply an extension of the nature of Babylon. Every structure on the plain and on the side of the mountain looked like the Babylon that Father had shown me.

Then He spoke again, "When Satan offered the nations of the world to the Son, he showed Him the Babylon you see now. Satan thought these man-made glories were a treasure the Son could not refuse. But the Son saw the work of men's flesh for what it was; wood, hay and stubble, and so has everyone who has completed the climb to the top of my Mountain. These shanties are the works of men, built by the wisdom of men, in order to make a name for themselves."

I queried again, "If this is Your mountain, how is it that they are building with wood, hay and stubble?"

He answered, "They do so because I am merciful and patient. I have sent many generations of prophets to warn them of the 'danger of their mixtures'. These places also serve the purpose of causing those who are truly seeking Me to recognize Babylon for what it is and choose to move up higher in their journey."

"'The Day' will reveal all men's works for what they are and that which is not of Me will be burned up; and that Day is now come upon mankind. In the days to come, Babylon will then serve as a gathering place for men's wisdom and works to be fully exposed, gathered together and burned up."

I had one more question, "So what is this Mountain?" He replied, "This is the place where heaven meets earth, where the Divine becomes 'one' with creation. This is the Mountain spoken of in the book of Daniel which dashes to pieces the nations of the earth and covers the whole earth. It is 'My Unshakable Kingdom'."

THE HOLY CITY

He continued, *"You have come to Mount Zion, to the heavenly Jerusalem, the city of the living God."* I dared to ask, 'If this is mount Zion, then where is the heavenly Jerusalem? I don't see any city.' It was then that I began to see His form clearly, and to my surprise Jesus Himself stood before me, I looked into His eyes and saw they had not changed; they were the same eyes of Love swirling with fire. To aid my recognition He said, "If you have seen Me, you have seen the Father. I AM one with the Father."

It was then that I noticed others gathered in robes of white on top of the mountain singing praise to God. Companies of angels surrounded these worshippers unified in worship to God. He said, "You can only see the New Jerusalem clearly when you see Me clearly. These sons and daughters gathered here ARE the New Jerusalem."

"They have BECOME the city prepared as a Bride for her Groom! This is my bride, the one whom I have chosen to become one with! I will dwell in and with her forever and my glory shall be seen in her and upon her." The contrast between what I had seen of the nature of the city below and the nature of the city above made me speechless. I allowed the full meaning of what I just heard begin to sink into my consciousness.

He said, "These are my witnesses who have 'overcome by the blood of the Lamb, and by the word of their testimony and have not loved their lives, even unto death'. These are my brothers and sisters, the sons and daughters of God who have chosen the Narrow Way and made the same journey you have made.

The number of overcoming witnesses is reaching completion. Just as at Pentecost 120 persevered until my coming, so I have kept a remnant that have persevered and overcome to bear witness to my coming Glory. I have been gathering unto Myself the first fruits of those who shall bear witness that the King has come and the Day of the Lord is here."

He then disappeared, but the sense of His presence and peace within me and around me was palpable and I knew He had not left me. I turned to behold the wonderful scene of complete unity of worship and adoration to God with the accompanying angels and my heart wept in praise to God! His Spirit spoke from within me, "Go and join them, you have a place among them!"

I stepped forward led by the Spirit to an open space between two worshippers and for a brief moment looked around and noticed a few I knew and loved, but there were fewer than I expected. It seemed that people from every race of mankind were joined together in a song of praise that rose higher and higher. I wept with joy and love toward my Father at the sound of it. I began to sing the deep crying in my heart, and it began to form into a song that fit in perfect harmony with those around me. Joy and peace like a river flowed from our hearts as the song continued.

Suddenly the Holy Spirit spoke within me and said, "Look around you!", so I looked around at the other people worshipping and saw a resemblance to Jesus in each one that I had not noticed before. I then looked into their eyes and saw the same swirling, fiery Love that I had seen before in both Father and Son.

Then, from within me, Jesus began to speak again, "The top of this Mountain is where heaven has already come to earth, where my 'will is done on earth as it is in heaven'; it is the merging place of these two realms."

"Those who have overcome and now abide on this mountain ARE in heaven and on the earth at the same time; and are now 'one' with heaven and with each other, even as I am one with my Father. But their 'oneness' is founded upon a greater truth; they have become one with me and my Father. It is through this 'oneness' with my Father and Myself that the people below will know that I have been sent of my Father and that you are my disciples."

Then Father Himself began to speak within me, "The day of my Son's coming is here, but it is beyond men's scope, understanding or ability to grasp how He is coming to mankind. The Holy City descending out of heaven comes as ONE with the Son and heaven, He is coming in and among the Holy City, the Bride, my sons, my witnesses."

"As they descend to the valley below, my Bride will bear witness with the Presence of my Glory in and upon them; first to those who are on the Mountain, and then to all upon the earth. All that is wood, hay and stubble will be burned up as Babylon falls in the face of my Glory. Even those who have seen by revelation what is about to transpire cannot fathom what is happening. It is beyond the ability of men to comprehend."

"As my sons go forth, this Mountain will cover all the earth, for it is my kingdom, and 'all the earth shall be covered with my Glory as the waters cover the sea'. The earth itself will be renewed as heaven and earth merges and becomes ONE because of my coming in and among my sons, and all that is not of me will be removed."

Suddenly, as if by a silent command, the sounds of worship ceased as the host of those in white stood side by side in perfect alignment and ready to move out on their heavenly quest. An angel put a trumpet to his lips and prepared for a blast. The Spirit within me cried, "Behold He Comes!!"

"Behold, I come quickly; hold fast to that which thou hast, that no one take thy crown. He that overcomes I will make a pillar in the temple of My God and he shall go out no more and I will write upon him the name of My God and the name of the city of My God which is the new Jerusalem, which comes down out of heaven from and with My God and I will write upon him My new name." (Revelation 3:11-12)

CHAPTER TWO

THE REVELATION OF ONENESS

After the revelation of the Mountain and the City, I received the following revelation from Father.

THE PLACE OF VISITATION

As was my normal daily pattern of worship and intimacy with God, I went alone to pray and pushed out of my mind all my wanderings of the previous day. I was blessed to realized that my newfound sense of Father's complete acceptance, that had overwhelmed me in the last week still remained. For some years now, whenever I had made a conscious effort to engage in intimate prayer, I would enter into a vision of a rooftop overlooking a city with the throne of my Father on the roof. I approached Him and we embrace once again, but this time without the nagging fear and doubt that had plagued me for years."

"Father then said something within my heart that shocked me; "You must no longer seek Me in this place of visitation on the rooftop! I am already within your spirit and always will be. You are also in my Spirit, just as I am in yours; so now I say to you to live from that place of ONENESS within you and commune with Me there."

"The place of visitation on the rooftop is the Secret Place where many of my children meet with Me, but that place is inadequate to fully change and deliver you from your doubts and fears, traumas, and brokenness. The place of my oneness within you is the place where we must commune because it is where I AM."

"It is only my Life in you that can overcome all things and change you. Your life must remain hidden in Mine, as I AM now your life. I told you before that I am doing something beyond the scope of man's understanding and that you were going to experience Me in a way you have not experienced me before; today is that day!"

ONE WITH GOD IN FULLNESS

Father continued, "Anytime you have walked by the Spirit in love my will has been done from this place of our 'oneness'. Anything you do that is of eternal value comes from Me dwelling within you. My work of reconciliation on the earth is in and through the agency of man as He yields, cooperates and allows Me to love the world through them."

"You have already walked as one with Me in part, but now you must walk as one with Me in fullness. This 'oneness' only comes through the perfection of my love abiding in you. He who is perfected in love does not function in fear, nor do they function from a place of duty or guilt. The measure of your love is the extent to which you have walked in 'oneness' with Me already."

"I dwell as one with those of my children who choose to live in my love, even as the Son walked in my love on the earth and was one with Me. There is only one commandment given as defined by the covenant I revealed through my Son, and that is 'to love one another as I have loved you'. "

"Those who cannot accept my love cannot love others as I love them and will be unable to reveal Me to my broken world. When you receive my unconditional love for you without consideration for your performance, it opens the door for you to truly love others unconditionally as I have loved you, a love not based upon men's performance."

"The doorway to 'complete oneness' opens when you truly believe in My love and quit hiding your wretchedness from Me in fear of judgment and wrath. Only then are you able to release others from your own judgments and love them as I do. While on the earth, my Son judged no one on His own. He simply submitted and chose to do and say what I was doing and saying (John 5:19)."

"You are free to walk in oneness with Me when you completely abandon your own life, opinions, judgments and perceptions of love to receive mine. The greatest hindrance to walking in oneness with Me is relying on your own judgments, understandings, feelings and opinions that you assume are Mine."

"My children, you still do not truly comprehend the boundless love I have for you and for all mankind. Everything I do, I do for and from my love, for I AM love. Even my judgments that seem unloving to men are for love's sake."

JUDGE NOT

"Many embrace concepts of biblical truth but have not embraced my perspective, which includes my judgment. I am simply looking for those who have abandoned their own lives and certainties and have chosen to receive Me as a child. It is in that child-like abandonment to my love and judgments that I will manifest Myself to them, in them and through them."

"The Son did not love the things of the world, and even though He left all judgment to Me, His perspective was the same as Mine and His judgments would also have been correct. Many form judgments that are not correct because they love the things of the world."

"You cannot walk in oneness with Me if you love the things of the world. If you love the things of the world then my love is not perfected in you and the oneness we should be sharing is limited to simple moments of visitation."

"The place of visitation has always been a path to the doorway of oneness; it has been a courtship of sorts. I have prepared and revealed Myself to you in this secret place through dreams, visions and angelic messengers sent to encourage, correct, and discipline you. But I want you to see that all of this has simply been to point you to Me, for knowing Me has always been the goal of this journey."

"You have come to know my heart and purposes as I have prepared you to be one with Me in a union of love. Dreams, visions, and angelic assistance are not going away; you have simply come to the place where you must now live from the place of intimacy and knowing me within you. You must walk with the mind of Christ; knowing my will, heart, and thoughts in every situation because your will, heart, and thoughts are one with Mine."

"When I sent my Son into the world, He walked in complete oneness with me; so much so that He said, 'If you have seen Me, you have seen the Father.' Everyone who truly believes in Me has the same potential or power to become One with Me just as the Son is one with Me. Those who are led by my Spirit just as Jesus was led by Me will manifest Me to the world just as Jesus did, for those who are led by my Spirit truly are my sons. In this place of oneness, the fullness of the great 'I AM' dwells in you; Father, Son and Holy Spirit."

A WITNESS TO ONENESS

"I have positioned you as one of many witnesses as to what I am doing in and through my people in this day. As I have told you before; the day of merely revelation has come to manifestation in my sons. What you write from my heart will bear witness with others and encourage them to find their destination in Me. The gifts are not going away, but the one who becomes one with Me will function in whatever capacity I deem necessary. Do not identify yourself simply as a gift to equip; your identity is in Me as my son, and my heart is simply that you establish that identity in others."

"The place of visitation and preparation can no longer help you as the doorway to oneness has been opened. Unless you choose to trust and walk with Me in oneness, you will shrink back into that former, lesser light. You will move back from intimacy to friendly acquaintance, a place where many who call themselves followers of Me remain."

"In this day I am raising up a generation of children who will not need to make the journey from religion to oneness as you have. They are being birthed into oneness as my sons. Indeed, many are even now being birthed outside the walls of religion into union with Me; and while they cannot see it now, they will need the wisdom of many like you who have fought the good fight for the freedom to walk as sons."

"For those of the previous generation who have believed and yielded to my preparation, their wilderness journey is now complete, the promised land is before you and now I will glorify Myself in and among my own."

MERGING OF HEAVEN AND EARTH

"Those who are one with Me are the New Jerusalem, the Bride. I have chosen to make my dwelling place both in and among them. Those in whom I dwell are my portals on the earth. They are my sons and the open heaven through which I express who I AM to all created things. Because they are IN Me, I am their access to the realms of heaven."

"It is because my sons are in Me and I am in them that the heavens and the earth are merging eternally. My sons are the meeting place of heaven and earth, and because they are seated in the Heavens in Me they are bringing the realities of heaven to earth. Heaven is simply this: Oneness with Me."

"Men often talk about 'going to heaven' someday, but my plan all along has been rather that heaven comes to earth. Heaven has touched the earth in part as my Spirit has moved in and through men. A remnant of my sons throughout history have become an open heaven for Me to touch the earth. The Power and Life from these past encounters with Me has served to progressively change my people and continue their maturing process throughout generations, changing the course of history itself. Few though have understood my moving and recognized Me in the midst of my blessings."

"These past moves became perverted by the wisdom and works of men who sought My benefits but did not seek to know Me fully in them and glory in Me. Religion separates man's knowing Me from my actions, benefits and blessings."

"Yet, I AM redemption, I AM Healing, I AM deliverance, I AM life, I AM grace, I AM truth, and I AM both the sustainer and sustenance of all creation. I AM consummating and restoring all things in heaven and earth, in Me."

POWERS OF THE AGE TO COME

Father then continued, "My Glory will overshadow you and the hearts of men will be laid bare before my glory. Men will either run in terror before Me, or they will humble themselves and be changed by my presence. This is the glory that many have prophesied about and my sons shall rise with my glory both in and upon them. I am conferring upon those who are one with Me the powers of the age to come. The gifts and anointing of my Spirit are only a 'taste' of the powers of the age to come."

"To be one with Me is to go from moving in the gifts and anointings which were but a shadow, to becoming the dwelling place of my glory. ***"Leaving the elementary teaching about the Christ let us press on to maturity", (Hebrews 6:1 NASB).*** You shall go from 'tasting' to 'feasting' and from 'receiving' to 'giving'. You have experienced supernatural knowledge and prophecy in part, but that which is in part is being done away with as that which is perfect has come."

"My sons will know, even as they are known. Where they are sent nothing will be hidden from them. All that is hidden in darkness will be exposed in my light. As Jesus knew the thoughts and intents of the hearts of men so you will too, not simply as a gift, but because you are one with Me.

You cannot love as I love until you see as I see. Knowing even as you are known brings perfection in my love, it requires you to love as I love. I will only entrust my discernment to those who use the knowledge of fallen men's hearts to bring redemption and not condemnation."

"My instruction to my children is simple – 'Pursue my love'. For the measure of authority and power you walk in is directly related to the extent to which your love has been replaced by my love. The more you love from my love, the more you will be enabled to express Me.

Many pursue obedience and fail to pursue my Love. Pursuing obedience apart from love is self-righteousness. The one who loves Me wholeheartedly does my will. Embracing oneness with Me enables you to be perfected in my love. Pursue love by continuing to embrace my love in oneness."

THE SABBATH DAY OF MY REST

"I am coming now in the fullness of time because I have found a people who will walk in oneness with Me as a corporate Bride. The Day of Mature Sons is upon you. Sons who will not labor by their own wisdom and works, but will choose Rest in my completed work, just as my Son did. It is the Age of my Heavenly Rest."

"The ages are not measured primarily in terms of time, but according to the state of my relationship with men. This unfolding age is named The Sabbath Day of My Rest. Those who become one with me have died in Me and have ceased from their labors and now enter my rest.

Those who have died in Me will know me as I AM. The I AM is now your life. See yourself as I see you. Because we are one, you ARE what I AM. You become my redemption, my healing, my deliverance, My grace and my life for the world. When we are one, I am free to touch people by your hands and feet; and you are my Word to them - 'as I AM, so you are in this world'."

CHAPTER THREE

THE TRUMPET BLAST

While contemplating the revelation of 'oneness' I had been receiving, I found myself back on top of the Mountain. I returned to a host of angels and worshippers standing in perfect alignment, waiting to move out at the Sound of the Trumpet.

THE WINGS OF AN EAGLE

Father spoke to me, "Son, you received the revelation of oneness with Me to prepare you to do my will when the trumpet sounds. You have begun to embrace oneness with Me as Christ is IN you. Christ in you also teaches you to abide IN Me. My abiding in you changes your nature into Mine. But when you abide in Me there is an exchange of your authority for Mine. To truly become one with Me, your nature must first be changed, enabling you to receive a change of authority. Those who are one with Me will rule and reign with Me."

"Oneness with Me is like the wings of an eagle. One wing is 'Me abiding in you', and the other is 'you abiding In Me'. I am in you, and you are in me. This happens when you choose to dwell by faith in the place in Me that I have prepared for you from before the foundation of the world. As I am in you and you are in Me, you soar like an eagle caught up in the heavenly up-draft of my Spirit. This 'oneness' will enable you to soar above the limitations, impossibilities and circumstances of life."

"Everything changes as you are caught up in a place of vision far above all principalities and powers that blind and bind mankind. It is time for my eagles to take their places In Me and fly higher and see more clearly than they have ever seen before."

SEEING WITH FATHER'S EYES

Father continued, "You have already seen the plain of humanity and its deep confusion from your own perspective. But now, as you are one with Me, I want you to see it with my eyes."

As I turned my gaze to the plain of humanity, I could clearly see one thing on the chaotic plain below: 'DESPERATE NEED!' So many people were busying themselves with activities in an attempt to fulfill their inner need; the need for love, security, acceptance, belonging and approval etc. But the most glaring need driving people was their lack of identity; nobody seemed to know who they were.

Men and women were drawn by their unmet needs into perversions, reckless lifestyles and the pursuit of fame, wealth, power and influence etc. These great primal motivations of mankind crashed upon me like a wave that took my breath away. Through tears of grief, I observed how men continued to build Babylon and trade with its goods and treasures in an attempt to fulfil their deepest needs.

Father then said, "Babylon is built upon the deepest unmet needs of mankind. Needs that can only be met in ME." As I contemplated the desperate plight of mankind, I shut my eyes and turned aside. The scene below me had completely changed from when I first stepped on the top of the mountain.

Father spoke in great tenderness, "The condition on the plain has not changed, it is your heart that has changed. When you first observed the chaos of the plain and the side of my mountain you held within your heart judgment, offense, and anger toward humanity."

"In your pride you harbored offense towards the world and those who claimed to know me yet wounded and opposed you out of their own unmet needs. This pride, judgment, and offense were the very things that kept you from oneness with Me and kept you from seeing people the way I do. When you died to your pride, judgments and offenses you were then able to see things through my eyes of love."

SPIRITS OF DARKNESS

His words impacted me deeply; I knew that I would never see things the same way again. Determined to see what He saw; I turned my gaze again to the plain below.

Unprecedented turmoil began to erupt as I now could see demonic spirits everywhere enticing and compelling people in their unmet needs to engage in wicked activities and lifestyles. Those who gave themselves over to wickedness became inhabited by evil spirits. Many of these people were placed by the evil spirits into positions of influence and power within Babylon. They were being inserted into politics, religion, economics, education and entertainment etc.

Father then spoke "The enemy's goal is very much like Mine. He is seeking people who will express his nature on the earth. When those he has enticed into perversions and self-seeking behaviors become the dwelling of evil spirits, they begin to express and take on the nature of the evil one, and then they are given authority to spread their wickedness to others."

I took in His words and continued to observe while a black, hazy fog formed across the plain. Those inhabited by evil spirits were gaining more power and influence and the atmosphere on the plain began to change. Men were deceived into thinking that darkness was light, addiction was liberty, and crushing your opposition was self-fulfillment. The darkness increased, as did chaos and violence.

It was then that I heard a cry! Under this oppression of darkness, I heard a heart-felt cry going out that went beyond inner need. It was a cry of bondage and suffering and my very being convulsed in grief. The pain overwhelmed me, and I sobbed in agony over the plight of man. "Oh Father!" I cried, "DO SOMETHING! Your children are being oppressed and destroyed, do something, oh God. Send me Lord! I will go!"

Father spoke, "My final preparation for you has been for you to see with my eyes and love with my heart. The evil one's ultimate goal is killing, stealing and destroying everything I have made. He desires to destroy mankind and the earth on which they live. I have heard the cry of my children and have seen their oppression and suffering. I am sending judgment that will bring deliverance, cleansing, and redemption."

THE INSTRUMENT OF JUDGEMENT

I asked, "How will You send Your judgment?" Father replied, "Behold my judgment!" I turned to look behind me and saw a great host waiting with the fire of God in their eyes.

He continued, "Here is the Bride, the New Jerusalem. She is my instrument of judgment on the earth. As the New Jerusalem descends onto the plain below, notice that she is not leaving this Mountain, but she is bringing it with her. Wherever she goes my rule will be established and my glory upon her shall judge and cleanse the inhabitants of the earth."

Jesus now began to speak, "Just as I was sent by my Father into the world to save it and not condemn it, so I am sending my Bride with redemption and restoration for whoever will receive it. My Bride comes to freely offer the water of life to whoever will let Me quench their needs. (Revelation 22:17)

But remember that I also came 'to destroy the works of the evil one', so I am sending those who are one with Me to execute on earth the sentence of judgment I have already pronounced from the heavens upon Babylon. You will release upon the earth what is already released in heaven and you will forbid on earth what is already forbidden in heaven. In this way, heaven is coming to earth." (Matthew 18:18)

The Father spoke again, "I have gathered my sons on this mountain as the first-fruits of the unfolding age, the initial mature harvest. You are my laborers being sent to work in the harvest field; you are my messengers of power. You are not going forth to harvest only, but to plant the incorruptible seed of Christ that bears fruit after its own kind. In fact, you ARE the seed; the sons of God!"

DECLARING THE VISION

I continued to gaze at the mighty army assembled around me. Father spoke, "Write down what you have seen and experienced and declare it to those assembled here. You are not speaking on your own."

As I began to speak another man came and stood beside me and together, we began to share the vision with people. Father then spoke, "By the mouth of two or more is the testimony established. You are witnesses to what I am already speaking to them."

Other witnesses then stepped forward and were also sharing the same vision among the people. These teams of witnesses began moving among His people by pairs, declaring with authority and clarity the revelation of the coming kingdom.

The unified vision brought clarity and purpose and began transforming those gathered on the top of the Mountain. The Glory of the Lord appeared over the congregation and the countenance of each began to change as the transforming glory inside each heart began to radiate externally from shining faces.

As we each then stood silent in our assigned places in complete unity, a sudden trumpet blast shook the ground ...

CHAPTER 4

INSTRUMENTS OF JUDGMENT

THE DESCENT

The blast of the trumpet was still ringing in my ears as we began to move out as one mighty army. As we descended from every side of the Holy Mountain we began to form into small companies of friends, whose hearts shared the same desires and dreams. After descending for a short time, the small company I had become knitted with began to see the first wood, hay and straw encampments that had been constructed closest to the top of the Mountain of the Lord.

Father spoke again, "Son, I am sending you first to these who have built closest to the top of the mountain. All of these camped on the side of my Mountain are captives. Most of them are born of my Spirit and all those born of my Spirit were born on the top of this mountain. Yet, almost all have been taken captive by what religion has built, just as you were at one time."

"Many were taken captive by religion on the very day they were spiritually born by well-meaning men and women who had already built or inherited these encampments on the side of my Mountain with man's wisdom and works. However, all those born of Me have been given an imperishable seed within, and wherever they have encamped there is within their hearts a deep inner longing for them to find their way to their true home, Me."

"I am sending my sons as deliverers; even as Jesus Christ was sent to destroy the works of the devil and set the captives free. I have told you that you are instruments of judgment; judgment first to my house and then to all of creation."

"I have given all judgment into the hands of the Son, Christ Jesus, and you are now become His hands and feet upon the earth. I am now going to show you what His judgment looks like. Turn around and see where you have come from."

THE COMING OF JUDGMENT

I turned to look where we had come from and with amazement realized that even after descending for a length of time, we were still standing on the level plain on top of the Mountain. We were nearly approaching the first encampments and were closer to the sprawling plain below then before, but we had still not actually left the top. I realized that the Mountaintop, and the Glory of the Lord resting upon it, was expanding to fill every place we went.

Father again spoke, "Every place you set your feet I have given to you. As I have told you before, 'This (Mountain) is the place where heaven meets earth, where the divine becomes one with its creation. This is the Mountain from the book of Daniel, which dashes to pieces the nations and covers the whole earth. It is 'my Unshakable Kingdom!' You have now come to dwell forever in this place and that place will be in you always. Judgment has now come to my house. Go forward to the first encampment and behold the judgment of Christ in His house. The angels have gone before you and prepared for your coming."

As I turned again to observe the encampments before us, a lady who was drawn to the atmosphere of heaven in which we stood approached and invited our small company to come to the gathering place where she and others were meeting.

We approached the encampment and entered the building where these gathered. The heavenly light of God's Mountain was dim and obscured by the enclosing structure that they had built. I was about to step forward and declare to those gathered there that what they had built was keeping the light of God from shining upon them. But suddenly Father spoke to me and said, "That judgment does not belong to you, it belongs to the Son."

Without warning, one of our company stood up in the dimly lit gathering and began singing a song of worship to Father. Without hesitation our company joined in the worship of Father in Spirit and Truth, lifting hands high and focusing our hearts upon Him. Most of those in the gathering quickly joined in with grateful hearts and the darkness began to subside. The light of God's glory began to emanate from within the worshipers as the Spirit of God began to move among the people.

The goodness of God began healing the spirits, souls and bodies of all those worshipping; causing them to shout for joy and weep in repentant gratitude. Every demonic oppression and religious mindset lifted off each person gathered and the room began to take on the heavenly glow we had experienced on the Mountain of His Glory.

The walls and ceilings began to shake as this Light increased and continued to surround and emanate from the worshippers. With a mighty crash and a shout of joy the worthless structure fell to the ground and burst into flames, completely consumed. Yet, its fall did not harm any of the worshipers. All the trappings of Babylon and its mixture were burned up in His holy fire.

The heavenly light shone unhindered and the place we were standing was now Holy Ground, the Mountaintop. We were filled with great joy, basking in His light and praising Him for His mercy and love. The sudden crash and ensuing glory caused some people to shrink back in great terror, as the reality of the presence of God shone a light in dark places and exposed the futility and smallness of their thoughts and deeds.

Some who had refused to enter into the spontaneous worship were both angry and outraged over the loss of what they had built, and they fled when the walls began to shake. They scurried down the mountain like the Israelites in the desert, fleeing the mountain of God's presence, not stopping until they were far from the top of the mountain. Some left the mountain altogether and wandered unto the broad plain below where Babylon sat enthroned. Jesus's great judgment had come!

THE EXPOSING LIGHT

Father again spoke, "Son, as you have observed, judgment is a good thing. Judgment is my love shining the light of my presence in darkness. This is the judgment; 'the Light has come' and there is nowhere to hide in the face of my presence. What is truly in every man is fully exposed in the light of my glory. If a heart is full of my love it will worship in my presence. If it is full of fear, anger, condemnation, judgment and hatred, all these attitudes will also be made manifest."

"When their primal condition is brought into my light, mankind will choose to either face the truth and turn to find true freedom or run away from the light. In my mercy, the removal of all mixture and darkness is made available to any willing to come into the Light."

"The light of my love will remove the mixture in the hearts of ALL those who call upon Me. It is my glory revealed in my sons that brings the judgement which is my eternal plan to set all things right."

I wept at the utter goodness of my Father. What love and grace had been revealed to my simple understanding! His judgment was not the condemnation of mankind swamped by their deception, lusts, hatred and fears as I had been taught many times. I had denounced, accused and attacked such men in their duplicity many times and never realized that my attitudes were the complete opposite of the Father's heart.

His judgment was simply to shine the Light of His goodness upon men and reveal Himself to them and in so doing reveal the true state of their own hearts without any criticism or anger. He had cast down the wisdom and works of men with His presence and His only desire was to set them free from their captivity and invite them into His kingdom. What a critical and angry fool I had been!

When I had completed my heart-felt pondering, He said, "Son, you've wasted time and effort opposing the religious systems men have built. I never called you to fight or defeat Babylon, I simply called you to come out from her!" I bowed my head once again.

"What men have built in my name is being judged and tried in the fire of my glory. What is built of Me will stand! If it is the wood, hay, and stubble of a religious system, it will fall and be destroyed. Each person must answer to Christ alone for the quality of their work. Every doctrine, opinion, tradition, certainty, theology and religious system of operation that has been sourced by men's wisdom and strength will end!"

At the mention of the wisdom and strength of men, I turned my gaze to the sprawling plain beneath the mountain and the city built upon the established wisdom and strength of men enthroned upon seven hills. I knew the Mountain of the Lord we stood upon was going to bring the demise of that wicked city, so then I asked Father a question, "What are those seven hills?"

THE MOUNTAIN AND THE SEVEN HILLS

"For who are you, O great mountain [of human obstacles]? Before Zerubbabel [who with Joshua had led the return of the exiles from Babylon and was undertaking the rebuilding of the temple, before him] you shall become a plain [a mere molehill]!" (Zechariah 4:7 AMPC)

Father responded, "Son, those are the hills that have been referred to by many as the seven mountains. They are the spheres of influence that are active among mankind and affect the life, culture, mindsets, society and behaviors of mankind. From man's perspective they are mountains. But, from my perspective they are only molehills."

"I am now placing my throne in the midst of the plain of humanity that lives and works upon those seven hills. Even now My Holy City is descending out of heaven to take Her place as the ruling city over all the earth, my city shall preside over those seven hills. My people are that city, which is the New Jerusalem, the Bride that 'has made herself ready' for her Groom, dwelling in oneness with Him for eternity. That plain, and the hills upon it, are your inheritance as joint heirs with Jesus Christ. In this transition of the ages, the Holy City has already begun to descend and expand His rule."

My gaze quickly turned again to the plain of churning humanity spreading out below the Mountain. In the midst of this sea of humanity was that large city already enthroned upon seven hills, Babylon.

I noted that there were skirmishes breaking out for the control of those seven hills, as diverse groups of every distinction had interest in controlling them. But it was the dark spirits which inhabited Babylon that determined who controlled the hills. These spirits positioned people on the hills to speak lies and deception into the worldly systems of politics, religion, family, economics, education, media, and entertainment.

As people came under the influence of these puppet-masters of evil, the dark hazy fog hanging over the plain became thicker and darker, further clouding men's vision. And then I saw that dark spirits goaded their subjects with a fury, for they could see the Light on the Mountain had begun to be empowered, expand, and descend.

FEAR, ANGER, AND OFFENSE

As I observed the valley falling into greater darkness, fear seemed to spread out over my head and fall down around my shoulders like a blanket. I began to wonder if anything could stop the fury of the evil and the people who gave themselves over as instruments of wickedness and deception. Then a rage over the unfairness and wrongness of it all came upon me, mixing with the fear. The thought screamed in my mind, "Something MUST be done!"

A tangible fear of the schemes of the devil, and a self-righteous rage over what was being done to Father's creation, began to war with the peace of God within me. In desperation I turned to Him in the place of peace within and cried "Father, help me!"

Supernatural peace suddenly burst forth within the core of my being, and the fear and rage dissipated like a cloud of mist blown away by a strong wind.

He spoke, "My son, when you focus upon the evil works of the enemy and what he is doing you become vulnerable to the dark fog of fear and anger. If you allow the fear and anger to find a place in you, you will be compromised and your rest in Me will turn to warring."

"You cannot remain on this mountaintop while in that state of un-rest. Remember how Moses allowed fear and wrath to overtake him and this heart of offense kept him from entering the Promised Land. Man's wrath CANNOT accomplish my purposes. Do not be offended by the world and its wickedness, for if you do so you will find that you have left MY Mountain. Keep trusting in Me and do not allow the offenses of anger, judgement and wickedness to take you captive."

"Many of my own have taken offense at evil of the world and its institutions. Many in their fear, anger, offense, and presumption take up the weapons of the world to fight for those very hills of influence you see on the plain below. Very few of my children have ever asked Me to reveal to them 'My plan of redemption for my broken, misguided world'. Look again with the faith I have bestowed upon you."

I turned my eyes to the plain again and to my utter surprise spotted a constant stream of warriors carrying weapons marching from the side of the mountain of the Lord to engage in battle for control of the hills. Father continued, "Some of my children have determined to ascend those hills and take control of them in their own strength, and by extension control the whole earth. They will not succeed this time, just as those who tried before them had failed."

"At one time the religion of Christianity took control of these hills and plunged much of the earth into the Dark Ages. At that time many left my Mountain, captivated by the lure of Babylon and the power to control life on the earth. Later, the Reformation marked a time when much blood stained those hills. Many of those who claimed to be Mine killed each other to be king of those hills."

"The resulting offense and the vile mixture of the world's attitudes within the church caused men to build the dwellings of Babylon on the side of this mountain you see today. They exchanged the authority of heaven for positions of power over the institutions of mankind. I never called my children to control those hills. I have a better plan; my Mountain, where my City rests, is coming to the plain! The authority of heaven is coming to fill the earth."

THE BASIS OF AUTHORITY

Father continued, "Man's control is the basis of the power the world wields. In contrast, the basis of authority on my Mountain flows solely from my Love. I have told you before; in my kingdom the measure of a man's love is the measure of his authority. 'Before the foundations of the world the Lamb was slain'; in this sacrifice of love, Jesus Christ established His authority over all creation from its very beginning."

"The basis of the authority of Babylon enthroned upon these hills is the power of human control and comes from man's wisdom and strength. But the 'foolishness of the cross is wiser than men's wisdom, and the weakness of the cross is stronger than men's strength'."

SONS REVEALED

"In the same manner that I sent Jesus to reveal Me to my people, thus I am now sending my revealed sons to My own house to make myself known as I truly Am."

"I have not sent you to judge men in your anger, but to be a resting place of my presence which shines the light of who I am in darkness. It is this light of my presence in you that reveals the hearts of men and scatters darkness."

"I am sending you to the plain of humanity in the same way, revealing Myself in my sons to all creation. It is the light of my goodness and love revealed in and through you that will drive away the dark clouds of wickedness. The wicked city enthroned upon the hills will fall with a mighty crash - not by the hand of man but through the glory of my presence in you. Upon those seven hills my city will shine with the light of my ever-increasing kingdom."

"I have shown you these things that you might have faith in the face of this offending darkness and to enable you to encourage your brothers and sisters when men full of wickedness prosper and enforce their will upon the peoples of the earth. You cannot fight a battle against the rulers of these seven hills with the weapons and wisdom of men or you will be soundly defeated. But 'with Me, ALL things are possible'. I go before you, and every place you set your feet I have given you. Do not fear! Trust in Me! Jesus the Christ has already overcome the world."

PART TWO
THE PATH TO ONENESS

CHAPTER FIVE

THE NARROW GATE

Some months after receiving my revelation of the kingdom of God coming forth as His Mountain, I received this encouraging teaching concerning the way Father wants to transform His people.

THE WROUGHT IRON GATE

As I was praying, I suddenly found myself standing on a narrow path leading off into the distance. As I scanned further, I could see the path stretched ahead into the dark night, leading to an unknown destination. As I walked along this path, I came upon a long line of people standing in the middle of the path. A man at the front of the line cried out, "You cannot go any further unless you enter the narrow gate!"

He stood before a narrow, wrought iron gate through which the people were attempting to travel. The top of the gate was fashioned from wrought iron and formed the words, 'The Narrow Gate'. This wrought iron banner was fastened so low down upon the gate that anyone desiring to enter had to crawl on their hands and knees to fit beneath it. I then noticed that those crawling were still required to squeeze between the narrow posts on either side.

I scanned the path beyond the gate and noticed that as far as I could see was what seemed to be a carnival of sorts stretched out along the narrow path into the darkness.

To my surprise I saw men and women positioned along the road shouting out instructions to the many souls traversing the road. It was as though they were presiding over a series of hurdles, doors, curtains and what seemed to be an obstacle course blocking the path. At each obstacle they would give instructions to those making the pilgrimage as to how to pass through the obstacle. Finally, I asked Father, "What is this gate and path with the obstacles all along the way?"

He replied, "This is the gate and the path of religion. These hindrances are the many stumbling blocks placed before my children by men. Religion is a stumbling block that places requirements upon men that I never placed upon them. It attempts to get men to pay or work or attend or study for what I have already freely given them in Christ."

I looked again to the path and saw that many of the obstacles were created and erected by the very ones giving out 'advice' as to how to overcome them. They had figured out how to turn the path of religion into an elaborate extortion scheme. They were receiving a return for their services in terms of money, honor, titles, attendance, and position etc.

Something was received from everyone in order to pass an obstacle. When they received the appropriate payment, the pilgrim would be rewarded with the 'secret' to overcoming, the 'keys' to unlocking hidden doors, the 'guidelines' on fasting and true worship, the 'steps' to spiritual success, the 'book' that was essential to future growth and so on and so on. All these purported to get you 'closer' to God, become more like God, be pleasing to God and get you to a place to receive His blessing or help you get to an upgrade to another spiritual level.

THE SUPERHIGHWAY

As I continued to gaze upon this religious charade, to my surprise I noticed that this 'narrow path', that at first seemed to be the only path, was simply one 'lane' of a much bigger super-highway that had many lanes on it. This road was very wide but it had hundreds of lanes with a multitude of people travelling in the same general direction.

I was being shown that each differing religion had established their own lane, with its own stumbling blocks for the people that adhered to their ideologies. But, equally, many of the other lanes were filled with people carelessly rushing down the road completely oblivious as to where they were headed. The lanes of the highway seemed to be divided between two different philosophies of travel:

One philosophy was religious engagement that lured people with levels of spiritual attainment and power. The other lured people with the philosophy that there was no absolute truth other than pleasing ones-self. One philosophy was rooted in striving to be like God through requirements and laws. The other philosophy was rooted in believing that man was his own god and no law existed. These two philosophies formed into two distinct streams of humanity flowing in the same direction, to the same destination, but were essentially on the same road.

Father spoke to me again, "This highway is so wide that those on the religious paths do not see that the lawless are on the same highway, headed to the same destination. These two philosophies are both manifestations of 'the tree of the knowledge of good and evil', yet they manifest differently. Religion manifests as a straight jacket demanding self-effort and self-righteousness. Lawlessness manifests itself as unchecked and unrestrained self-indulgence and self-expression. But son, I only showed you this highway to show you The True and Narrow Gate."

THE FOUNTAIN OF LIFE

As He finished speaking, a light shone brightly from behind me and cast my shadow alongside the superhighway. Then a voice 'as of many waters' spoke from behind me saying "Turn around!" I turned to look and there stood Jesus shining in brilliant light. He was standing in the midst of a large fountain of water and water flowed out from His belly. As His voice thundered, the waters rushed out with greater force and spread across the ground. "I AM the narrow gate. I AM the way! He who drinks of Me will never thirst again!"

I immediately fell to my knees in worship and began drinking from His fountain of life. An overwhelming joy I had never felt before burst from deep within me and I lost track of all time as I basked in His goodness and love. I awoke as if from a dream in a state of heavenly bliss and saw a bright light, like the noonday in summer.

I found myself standing among a small gathering of people and realized that the light was not coming from the sun but emanating from the people standing with me. Even more shocking was seeing the water flowing from everyone's belly, including my own. The water flowed in the same manner as the fountain that I had seen flowing from Jesus' belly.

When people spoke, the fountain within them welled up with a greater flow that quenched the thirst of everyone around them and bathed them in light. I saw that the water was also the source of this light. As it flowed from within each person it caused the body from which it flowed to emanate His light.

I turned around to see the superhighway and to my joy and amazement many of those on the road nearest us had been drawn by the light were on their knees scooping up and drinking the water as it flowed down around the small group gathered there.

COME AND DRINK

I quickly joined them and began offering water freely to any willing to drink. Many who received the water were weary and downtrodden, but when they drank the Living Water the transformation that came upon them was swift and complete. In a moment sorrow turned to joy, anxiety to peace and fear to love.

I also noted that as the people were transformed, the water also began to overflow from their bellies flowing out to be freely received by other thirsty souls. To as many as received what was offered, the water of life transformed them and kept on flowing.

As we continued to offer this living water to all who would receive it, the people began to mob the water-bearers for a drink. As a result, the explosion of light on the superhighway caused many people to stop their journey to investigate what was happening 'over here'. The light began to shine so brightly that the darkness shrouding the highway began to lift and it was clear to most that it led to an ominous precipice before a deep chasm. Anyone going over it would plummet into darkness.

Again, Father spoke to me, "Son, the stingy requirements of religion are not the path to life. Nor is it to be found in simply pleasing oneself. Jesus IS the narrow gate, Jesus IS the path of life, Jesus IS the light and Jesus IS the living water of life. All who drink from Him will never thirst again but live." (John 4:14)

"The gateway to life is not narrow because it is hard to enter; it is narrow because Jesus is the ONLY way to life. You must cease from your religious labors to enter by Him, through Him and into Him. 'His yoke is easy and His burden is light and you will find rest for your souls in His life-giving flow'." (Matthew 11:30)

"Only from Him, in Him and through Him can you obtain the everlasting life I made available for mankind. All who choose to drink of Christ Himself will receive the fullness of the abundant life I offer; not someday, not through hard work, not through any religious activities, but NOW from my outstretched hands!"

"Men will either trust in what is already finished by embracing and receiving abundant life of Christ, or they will follow another road which only leads to darkness. 'The Spirit and the Bride say come and drink' of this abundant new life."

CHAPTER SIX

THE MINISTRY OF RECONCILIATION OR OFFENSE

"As therefore the tares are gathered and burned in the fire, so shall it be in the end of this age. The Son of man shall send forth his angels, and they shall gather out of his kingdom all things that offend..." ~Jesus~ (Mathew 13:40-41)

The end of this Age brings with it a purging. The purging is of everything that is causing offense. It also brings a healing for those who have been taken by offense as they allow Father to release to them healing and grace. The sad fact is that those who are offended can easily become offenders themselves. Father has great mercy and is bringing a move of repentance and reconciliation to the earth.

It is a time for those who have been offending to repent and change, and those who have suffered from deep offense to receive their healing into wholeness. We are about to see a move of the Holy Spirit that will bring deep repentance and healing to people's hearts. Today is the 'day of salvation' and of complete restoration to intimacy with Father and to all our brothers and sisters.

Jonah prophesied to the citizens of Nineveh saying, *"Yet forty days, and Nineveh shall be destroyed.!",* and yet the city was not destroyed. Is it possible that Jonah spoke the prophetic word excluding the option to repent because of his own offense toward Nineveh? Jonah had no love for the Ninevites and was angry when they repented and God did not destroy them.

*"And he prayed unto the LORD and said, I pray thee, O
LORD, was this not what I said when I was yet in my country?
Therefore I hastened to flee unto Tarshish, for I knew that
thou art a gracious God and full of compassion, slow to anger, and
of great mercy, and dost repent when thou art come to take
punishment." (Jonah 4:2)*

THE MINISTRY OF OFFENSE

It is easy for us to vent our frustrations in the name of the Lord.
One of the greatest sources of false or tainted ministry is offense. I
may reject or closely judge a 'word' that has been given when I
sense offense that is not resolved. For example, many who speak the
destruction of the institutional church and its people are still
harboring bitterness toward those who have hurt them within it.

While God is destroying the system of religion in the
institutional church, do not ever forget that He is destroying a
system and loves people. Remember that 'the battle is not against
flesh and blood ...' Many have forgotten or never really understood
that He hates the bondage of controlling systems placed upon men
but loves the people within them. There will be those who suffer
loss within the system by refusing to change, but we rejoice in
Babylon (the controlling system) falling, not the suffering of people
that Father loves 'with an everlasting love'.

This mixture of offense happens frequently in political, national
or globally significant prophecy. People do not realize that they
tend to prophesy from their own agenda when they have not
resolved to flow from the place of Rest in the Lord in a particular
arena and speak from an offended heart.

It is easy to prophesy gloom and doom when you are angry at
your political leaders or offended at a nation that opposes the
nation you love. So many believers seem to be convinced that God
is a member of the political party they support.

If you are offended by Islam, it is easy to rejoice over the death of Bin Laden rather than rejoice in the salvation of Muslims. Offense is a snare that corrupts, infects, and twists our perspectives and attitudes.

Jonah's problem was not simply being too stubborn to go to Nineveh, he was deeply offended and angry because of the centuries old evil done to his people by the Assyrian kings of Nineveh. Even after obeying God, he did not want Him to forgive the Ninevite's, he wanted them all dead!

SPIRIT OF BITTERNESS - THE ENEMY

Bitterness is the state of unforgiveness and or woundedness in one's heart that is the direct consequence of taking offense in the past. This bitterness has the potential to turn a true prophet into a false prophet and turn a mature son back into acting like a religious man.

Jonah struggled with this bitterness as his people had suffered severely at the hands of the people of the Assyrian Empire. It took a mighty act of God to get him to finally speak the word of the Lord, and even after that he still hated them. Jonah did not know the true foundational nature of the God he served – Love.

If you are offended by a spiritual leader, political leader, a nation, a particular religion, or anyone else for that matter, regardless of how evil they are and how badly you have suffered at their hands, your actions and attitudes will be controlled and distorted by this spirit of offense. A lot of criticism and judgment directed toward religion and its leaders, toward political leaders, and other people groups, are sourced in bitterness rooted in offense taken in the past.

"And then shall many be offended and shall betray one another and shall hate one another. And many false prophets shall rise and shall deceive many. And because lawlessness shall abound, the charity of many shall wax cold." ~Jesus~ (Matthew 24:10-12)

This verse describes the state of much of the church in these days of the closing of the Age. Many have taken offense at the hypocrisy of religion. The ranks of atheists and agnostics are filled with offended men and women who have become deeply bitter at those representing Christ who have acted like the devil himself.

The 'out of church' movement's numbers have been swelled with disenchanted, wounded and deeply offended people who were given a raw deal in the halls of religion? Thousands of offended individuals have stopped going to any form of church altogether. Also, heresy-hunting 'ministries' are motivated by and continue to sniff out sin and offense from a 'church' acting like the world.

LOVE, THE ONLY REMEDY FOR OFFENSE

Offense at the actions and words of others has been a tool that Father has used to expose within my own heart the deeply hidden places of pride and self-centeredness in me that were not obvious until I encountered offense suffered at the hands of others.

The Spirit of God told Ananias concerning Paul, *" ...for I will show him how much he must suffer for My name's sake." (Acts 9:16 NASB)* To be used for the greater purposes of God demands suffering offense at the hands of others and meeting it with the unconditional love of God. Jesus's ministry shows us multiple situations when He refused to take offense and chose to love and forgive those who slandered, accused, despised, and even tried to kill Him.

At the cross we see the ultimate example; where Christ Jesus laid down His life in love for those who hated Him. And it is at the same cross of suffering offense with love that all who would follow in His footsteps today must bear.

There is a glory in suffering offenses with the unconditional love of God that releases in us a joy that is unspeakable. I have responded wrongly to the attacks of others upon me or my family many times. In the midst of that offense and ensuing bitterness; Father has been faithful to show me the places of self and pride that has been the "landing pad" upon which the offense of others has landed.

The times I have responded correctly have been through choosing to respond to offense with unconditional love. Two experiences come to mind from the past in which the Holy Spirit turned the opportunity to be bitter and offended into healing for me and released love for the offender in my heart.

In a business dealing by which I was losing income due to the refusal of a Christian to abide by our agreement; I was led to fast for forty days. This fast was not for my sake, but for the physical and psychological healing of the man who was responsible. In the end I recovered most of my losses and had property restored to me, but only after taking my eyes off myself and showing real love and kindness to him personally and in prayer.

Another instance concerned someone who was personally and very grievously an offense to my family and continued in their sin. In that situation I was moved by the Holy Spirit to approach the man and tell him that though I did not agree with what he was doing, I loved and forgave Him because God loved and forgave me. Through that step of faith, I received profound healing and deliverance from woundedness and bitterness.

FATHER'S GREAT LOVE

"But I say unto you, Love your enemies, bless those that curse you, do good to those that hate you, and pray for those who speak evil about you, and persecute you…" ~Jesus~ (Matthew 5:43-44)

There are times we must make a clear choice to love and pray for someone who is offending us. It is Father's love alone that can release us from offense. It is His love alone that 'covers a multitude of sins'. It is His love alone that washes us free from the root of bitterness that can grow up and defile many. Father is looking for a people who will choose to not be offended by the sin of individuals, those in the church and the actions of many in the world; and be His light of love to them.

But we must first embrace and acknowledge the Love our Father has for us and all of His children. We must 'offer ourselves as living sacrifices' to Him and embrace His great love for us that brings healing and forgiveness for others.

It is vitally important to engage with our heavenly Father and trust in His love and goodness so we can receive the healing we need from Him. His Love alone brings healing to release us from our state of self-deception. In His unconditional love, there is a glory that changes our perception of Him and of our brothers and sisters. He wants to impart to us a love built on brokenness for people, and a love that lays down our lives for those who may even try to kill us.

DREAM: THE CRITICAL MAN AND HIS FOLLOWER

I had a peculiar dream in which I was in my home and a man who had criticized and accused me of being a false prophet came and sat down in my easy chair. I began to confront him concerning the inappropriate way he was criticizing me. He got up and disappeared into a television screen where he was unable to hear my concerns.

Again, he appeared in my house and disappeared as he went into the television again. Then, another man followed him into the television. I thought I could do the same thing, so I went to the television and was able to get my head and upper body into it. Then, a feeling of deep unease overtook me, and I pulled myself out before I became very sick. I suddenly realized it was wrong for me to follow what these others had done. I then realized that the two men were now trapped in the television and were unable to get out.

I responded by getting onto my knees and prayed to Father for mercy to deliver these two men. Immediately they were freed. I saw that they were no longer in the house, but outside. They were no longer given access to the house because of their critical spirit. I then went outside to the men and said with a very sobering tone, The Holy Spirit says: ***"Don't do that again! I love you - but don't do that again!"***

NO TOLERANCE FOR THE CRITICAL SPIRIT

My dream of men coming into my home and sitting in one of my chairs represented how a critical person can come in and steal or take someone's place, their seat of rest and specific areas of spiritual responsibility. A tell-a-vison can only project a viewpoint to you, it cannot relate or receive anything from you.

A critical person cannot hear and receive from others but is focused on making their own opinion or view known. Critical individuals are trapped (in bondage in the television) in this mindset, being unable to hear or be teachable, and only give opinions from their critical perspective. It is a temptation when you are criticized to start criticizing others back; just as I 'entered into' the tell-a-vison for a time becoming like the two critical persons.

Our Father is willing and able to free us from criticism, but critical individuals are not allowed access in the house with seats of responsibility or authority they have no right to be seated in. The warning, given twice, means Father has determined that this critical behavior will not be tolerated.

STAYING WITHIN YOUR PLACE OF AUTHORITY

It is not wrong to recognize and disdain behaviors and attitudes that are evil. Years ago, I heard a man speak who was a guest speaker at a famous ministry just before the leader was exposed for sin and deception. Father told this man that the leader was in sin and He was judging him, but He did not let him confront the man. He only showed him his sin and deceit.

Why? Father showed me he was not given a place of responsibility for the spiritual state of the ministry which would have given him the authority to confront him. The right to confront has at its core the work of the Holy Spirit, who alone gives responsibility with the authority to confront. To confront without the legitimacy of Spirit directed responsibility inherently brings harm and does not carry Spirit led authority and conviction.

Thus, trying to confront someone or something that is beyond our sphere of authority and responsibility can inadvertently bring forth a critical spirit. We must know when we have been given the authority and responsibility by Father to confront with correction, lest it turn from correction to criticism.

GODLY CONFRONTATION

The authority to confront is the sole domain of the one given responsibility, not the one who is offended by sin, rejection, or false doctrine. Godly confrontation from a kingdom of God perspective will never flow from a heart of criticism.

The Father's heart is only ever motivated for reconciliation. It is a responsibility given by Father to preserve, protect or purify within one's sphere of spiritual influence. We only have the authority to confront in the spheres of influence where we have been given personal responsibility by Father Himself.

For example: in a situation where someone is a known sexual predator and is trying to get to my children, I will confront them to protect my own. I will also confront and correct my children if they are walking down a path of wrongdoing that will lead to their destruction. The same responsibility to confront applies in the kingdom of God. Men and women have authority in whatever sphere of responsibility God has given them; to confront both evil and error, be it their home, spiritual setting, or business.

NO MORE TOLERANCE

Much of the problem with criticism in the church comes from those trying to correct people over whom they have received no spiritual responsibility or relationship of trust, and more importantly, have no direct leading by Father to do so. Confrontation, when led by the Holy Spirit, is done with an understanding of one's own weakness 'in fear and trembling'.

Criticism's root is pride in one's own knowledge or perceived superior spirituality. Criticism makes judgments apart from Father's heart and His pure intent to restore and make whole.

Criticism can also be an attempt to lift oneself up through finding fault in others. Anyone holding unforgiveness, faultfinding, accusation or a critical spirit will not enter the kingdom of God. I pray that Father gives us eyes to see any place in us where a critical or accusing spirit has been allowed to defile and derail His purposes for our lives.

JUDGING ALL THINGS - VERSUS FINGERPOINTING

Passing judgment is solely the domain of our heavenly Father. But as his children we are to judge or discern things constantly as it pertains to people and situations. The ability to make judgments (discern) is an aspect of being created in the image of God.

There are two types of judgment: false judgments made by the soul of man, and righteous judgments inspired by the Holy Spirit within. True Spirit-inspired correction is long overdue in the ecclesia, but we will not be able to bring correction without repenting of all attitudes of false judgments first.

There is a massive difference between 'finger pointing' and speaking the truth by the Holy Spirit that confronts or convicts. The church has for so long passed judgment according to the flesh, that they have confused true correction with the finger pointing of men. Finger pointing causes division. It is the nature of the accuser to expose the errors and weakness of others through finger pointing. You cannot speak a Spirit-truth that confronts and convicts if you are still finger pointing. Our Father desires to teach us to walk in righteous discernment from hearts cleansed of finger pointing.

There is a difference between the pure in heart who have simply been taught false doctrine and practices, and those who are promoting, teaching, and proselytizing with false doctrine or practices from a root of self-interest. We should not be harshly censoring and correcting people with pure hearts who are seeking to know God but are still on the journey out of religion.

While not compromising truth; we must learn to honor and give grace to brothers and sisters who are pure of heart. Yet we must also know by the Holy Spirit what must not be tolerated in the ecclesia, and we must not fear to confront on the level of public or private platform upon which it is promoted. If evil seed is spread broadly, it must be dealt with broadly.

Paul confronted Peter in front of the whole assembly because it was in a very public manner that Peter was promoting falsehood, as revealed in Galatians 2:12-14. Yet when a brother sins against us personally, we are simply asked to go to them privately (see Matthew 18:15). Thus, we see that Paul, led by the Holy Spirit, only addressed falsehood in spheres of influence given him by God and did not meddle in the spheres of others.

WHEN NOT TO TOLERATE

"'But I have this against you, that you tolerate the woman Jezebel, who calls herself a prophetess, and she teaches and leads My bond-servants astray so that they commit acts of immorality and eat things sacrificed to idols." ~Jesus~ (Revelation 2:20 NASB)

The Jezebel that Jesus judged in His letter was not a spirit. A spirit is not given time to repent the way Jesus gave this Jezebel in Revelation 2. Jesus was confronting a real flesh and blood person who was leading God's people astray. This Jezebel is an example of what must not be tolerated in the body of Christ; 'those who teach others to lead them astray'. God does not tolerate these, nor will He let the church tolerate them.

In nearly every case of error or sin that needs confronting there are a few constants I have seen, though it may not be limited to these. These relate to instances of either legalism or the license of lawlessness. These are manifestations of the tree of the knowledge of good (legalism) and evil (license).

Legalism is any requirement or demand that we place upon men that is not a directive of the Holy Spirit. The requirement to follow religious rules, to be part of a membership to be in fellowship, to submit to the control of others, etc. All of these are laws placed upon people that rob them of their Godly inheritance, namely maturing into their inheritance as fully formed spiritual beings, 'in Christ'. These are not God's requirements, but the doctrines of men or devils.

License of lawlessness is the unrestrained pleasing of self, which manifests as Paul writes to the believers in Galatia: "***Now the deeds of the flesh are evident, which are: immorality, impurity, sensuality, idolatry, sorcery, enmities, strife, jealousy, outbursts of anger, disputes, dissensions, factions, envying, drunkenness, carousing, and things like these, of which I forewarn you, just as I have forewarned you, that those who practice such things will not inherit the kingdom of God. (Galatians 5:19-21 NASB)***

We are soon going to understand more completely why God, being Love incarnate, is 'Holy, Holy, Holy'! His love brings holiness for our own good. There is no peace with these destructive self-serving things or the people who promote them. These influences defile and diminish the Life of Christ in His people, and while they continue to be tolerated, all aspects of the life of His children 'in Christ' are diminished both in the individual, and in any group of believers. Not tolerating those who place these shackles of legalism or license on His children is the expected stance for the body of Christ.

When error or sin is allowed to spread within a group, the level of spiritual power and spiritual discernment plummets to the point where people are not able to recognize what is of the flesh and what is of Spirit. This loss of spiritual power and vision is the price paid for tolerating false doctrines, false practices, and immoral behavior.

PART THREE
'COMMON-UNION'

CHAPTER SEVEN

BE THE FAMILY OF GOD

THE MINISTRY OF RECONCILIATION

I must confess I have received a profound heart change and done much repentance lately. Many have been waiting for a kingdom outpouring that will sweep the nations. I tell you without question that when it comes, it will ONLY be revealed in its fullness when it is released as a 'Wave of Love', laying down its life for others.

I am not impressed with prophesies, doctrines, and gifts, but rather, I am impressed with one's ability to tear down the strongholds in the hearts of men with transforming Love!"

If we are not a true and living expression of Father and His kingdom, what good does it do us to preach the kingdom? I do not know about you, but I am done with pointing of the finger. I am done with ruminating on the wrongs done me by the 'organized church' and its leaders.

I am rather choosing to lay my life down for religious men. I will cry out REPENT! But it will not be with a heart of anger over the way in which I have been treated, it will be with a heart of brokenness for the way in which the enemy has killed, stolen and destroyed the people of God.

There are men and women of God, who have persevered for years, that have been extremely faithful in what they have been given to do and yet they are still held in a serious measure of bondage to religion. I have been moved often by the Holy Spirit to love and honor people such as these. I have seen that by dishonoring them through finger pointing and speaking accusingly of their lack of understanding, I have done absolutely NOTHING to further the kingdom of God, in fact quite the reverse.

While I cannot build the way others are building, or what they are building, I can build with what measure of relationship and trust they are willing to agree to. God is building with love and relationship – so can I do any differently? Religion is sadly building a structure that will inevitably fall. Come, let us build with love, and when the walls of religion fall, His structure, built with Love, will be a place of refuge for all.

A TURNING OF HEARTS, A TURNING OF THE PAGE

We must lay down ALL that we have known, perceived, been taught, and are certain of to embrace what is of value to God. In the face of Father and His great love we are wise if we choose to approach Him as unfaithful prodigal sons, knowing that He receives us unreservedly as we come to Him with faith 'as a child'. The ensuing days will be as if we had awakened from a dream, when 'we will forget the former things, for the new things have come'.

"When the LORD shall turn again the captivity of Zion, we shall be like those that dream. Then our mouth shall be filled with laughter and our tongue with singing; then they shall say among the Gentiles, The LORD has done great things with them. The LORD has done great things with us, of which we shall be glad. Turn again our captivity, O LORD, as the streams in the south. Those that sow with tears shall reap with joy. He that goes forth and weeps, bearing the precious seed, shall doubtless come again with rejoicing, bringing his sheaves with him. (Psalm 126)

Father says, "Now is the day of my healing, now is the day in which those who revere and honor Me shall go forth in freedom, 'leaping as calves who have been kept in a stall', but now are freed. The time of affliction and infirmity of my beloved one has ended; the 'Day of the Lord' is at hand."

Father says, "I have seen your perseverance through facing your weaknesses and your trials, and I now move my hand on your behalf. The world will tremble, the powers will all be shaken, but my name in your midst is a strong tower." Great healing is coming to the Father's own.

"But for you who fear My name, the sun of righteousness will rise with healing in its wings; and you will go forth and skip about like calves from the stall." (Malachi 4:2 NASB)

HEALING IN COMMUNION

While I have experienced healing in many ways in my life, Father has made it clear that for myself and many others another level of healing from the effects of the fall is coming in embracing 'common-union' with others. Oneness with God inevitably brings oneness with others. There is a fullness of restoration and healing individually and corporately that is ONLY found in communion with others in the body.

It has always been the will of God that Christ would be fully known in His body, and that the glory of God in Christ is being revealed in us corporately. Therefore, we are complete in Him, and we are also ONE 'in Him', in communion with others. Their strengths and graces 'in Him' are then freely available to us in true fellowship-relationships. Furthermore, what He has given us is made available to others as the Life Blood flows and healing comes to the rest of the body. Thus, we receive Him when we fully accept and see Him in others!

There is an awareness coming when we shall lose the distinction as to what is Him and us. This comes as we continue to engage in and be aware that we are ONE with Him. How many have truly entered the wonder of the experience 'I no longer live but Christ lives in me'? There is a healing of spirit, soul, mind and body that is about to burst forth like a dam that has been blocked for nearly an age.

The healing coming forth is a result of His children returning to Him and returning to common-union with each other as members of his body. Christ is coming to us in fullness as we receive Him and the portion He is releasing through His people. Truly, our 'communion' of fellowship is in His blood and we are part-takers of His body. For His blood courses through the veins of His body bringing life to the separate members. As we come together unified IN HIM, healing and life is flowing.

"The cup of blessing which we bless, is it not the fellowship of the blood of the Christ? The bread which we break, is it not the fellowship of the body of the Christ? For one loaf of bread means that many are one body, for we are all partakers of that one loaf. (I Corinthians 10:16-17)

DISCERNING THE BODY

We must clearly separate from that which is NOT Him, but we are expected to be ONE body corporately, just as we become ONE with Him individually. When the body has a severed part, the blood does not flow, and the severed part begins to die. The weakness and sickliness that have come from not 'discerning' His body is ceasing, as He ends the division and 'cutting off' of the true members of His body.

"For he that eats and drinks unworthily, eats and drinks judgment to himself, not discerning the Lord's body. For this cause many are weak and sickly among you, and many sleep." (I Corinthians 11:29-30)

We cannot hope to truly discern in the flesh those that are of Him and those that are not. But by the Holy Spirit we can discern and know, apart from doctrinal agreement and diversity of gifts and callings, those that are in Him.

I was given a prophetic word through this scripture: *"Then you will call, and the LORD will answer; You will cry, and He will say, 'Here I am.' If you remove the yoke from your midst, The pointing of the finger and speaking wickedness, And if you give yourself to the hungry And satisfy the desire of the afflicted, Then your light will rise in darkness And your gloom will become like midday. (Isaiah 58:9-10 NASB)*

I have personally been moved by the Holy Spirit to expend my energies on behalf of those hungry for truth and meeting the needs of those oppressed by religion. As I have written, Father is delivering me from the need to 'point the finger' at the failings of others and instead, build bridges of 'common-union' with all who are in Him.

We have transitioned into a 'New Day' where operating our gifts in isolation falls short of the glory that He wants to reveal to us, in us and through us. There is a love that is in the Holy Spirit that compels those who are truly His to unite. I have been shown that it is this alone that will break down the great barriers between believers and allow the necessary healing to flow. Let there be a healing flow from Him – 'let it begin with me, Lord'.

"I pray that Christ may make His home in your hearts through your faith; so that having your roots deep and your foundations strong, in Love, you may become mighty to grasp the idea, as it is grasped by all God's people, of the breadth and length, the height and depth; yes, to attain to a knowledge of the knowledge-surpassing Love of Christ, so that you may be made complete in accordance with God's own standard of completeness." (Ephesians 3:17-19, Weymouth)

Thus, Paul relates our completeness in Christ to understanding and apprehending different dimensions and aspects of Christ in the fullness of the breadth and the length, the height and the depth of His love.

Years ago, Father revealed this truth to me while studying CAD (Computer-aided design). I was taught that it takes at least three viewpoints (perspectives) to have a complete representation of the dimensions of any structure. Those dimensional views are: the top view, the side view and the front view.

The different members of His body also have differing perspectives and expressions of Christ that portray only a portion of the complete revelation of Christ. I believe Father has PURPOSELY withheld the full revelatory measure from us individually, so that we can only grasp it fully when we are in mutual love and submission to one another within the family of God.

As Paul revealed to the Ephesians, we will only receive the fullness of Christ in the unity of the faith – *"…until we all come forth in the unity of the faith and of the knowledge of the Son of God unto a perfect man, unto the measure of the coming of age of the Christ: (Ephesians 4:13)*

The 'fullness of the measure of the stature of Christ' is even now beginning to be manifested in us, as we step into the unity of the faith with those God has purposed that we become joined to in Spirit. I have come to know that as I receive insight, correction, impartation, encouragement, and truth from others in God ordained relationship, alignment, and connection; I receive of the Spirit of Christ and receive a greater measure of completion.

What each member has personally received could well be a missing piece of the puzzle for another in the ecclesia who needs what only they have to give. In this unity of mutually receiving of Christ in each other there is a powerful release of His Spirit as the full revelation of His nature and authority is released in and through individuals.

FORCEFUL SPIRIT FLOW

In the early morning hours last week, I received a vision of a crashing wave of water like a forceful unleashed river from a burst dam. It demolished a structure that had an outer shell like a water tower. It completely demolished the structure and I saw the word 'shell' as a caption below the structure. I did not receive full understanding of this vision until sharing it in communion with two brothers from the east coast on a Skype call.

One brother saw in the Spirit that this was the released power of the Holy Spirit unleashed as a result of the joining of the family of God in common-union. I then came to see it as a breaking through the shell of the man-made structures in a corporate sense, and the removal of the shell or mask of false identity we have built personally. This breaking-open is both good and shocking for us as we see what is truly living on the inside of us.

What is inside will truly be exposed, released and identified for what it is. As the shell of man's pride, self-will and false identity are being uncovered and removed, so the restraints of fear and flesh that have hindered the expression of who Christ is 'in us' are being destroyed. All that was constrained within the hard shell must be released to become part of the mighty rushing river. This is happening across the globe, and its powerful force will not be abated by man.

Entering His ordained plan of COMMUNION in Christ with others releases a fullness and a Spirit flow that destroys the hardened outer shell of religion and inhibition in His people. This unity that releases power is found in Christ alone. It is not the false unity centered in attachments to the organizations, doctrines or leadership structures of the past. These false sources of unity are in fact the 'shell' I saw in my vision and MUST be demolished!

Father is uniting us all as brothers and sisters of Christ in a Family. This flow has begun, and will demolish the hardness of heart that religion, pride, self-will and offense has placed around the hearts of God's children.

WE ARE FAMILY

My part simply is but one piece of a whole that when brought together with others in the family of our Father forms a clearer, more complete expression of Christ. I have operated for too long 'on my own' and have seen how the lack of common unity has kept me from receiving and apprehending more fully the Christ life I am called to.

Maturity is about growth. We must recognize that spiritually, growth is about receiving and being transformed by what we have not known. It is important to know that what others may have received is not necessarily what we have received. Fullness of understanding and life is available in God ordained and established relationships of giving and receiving.

To be sure, there is deception and falseness that all of us must come out of as we receive further truth God has given to others, but Father has a way of removing those blinders in relationship. If you cling to knowledge that may be even true at the expense of relationship, you can miss the TRUTH Himself. His desire is that in unity we express the fullness of who He is in completeness as His family on earth. It is about a heart attitude of teachableness that is willing to receive from the least likely source.

THE WINE AND THE WINESKIN

'It is death to have a wineskin without wine, but it is loss to have wine without a wineskin. We must have the wineskin AFTER we have the wine.' ~Watchman Nee~

When we experience the wine of God's love it is easy to enjoy the wine and not give a thought to the structure that contains it. I have interacted with some that want to revel in the nature of God and resist being contained within a wineskin in fear of the abuses of the past.

It is important to recognize and reject false religious structures that are burdensome and complicated. Yet, while the most important thing is our love relationship, which is the essence (wine), we need both the wine and the wineskin to preserve the wine. Father always makes provision for both.

Fathers' wineskin is not a business, a religion, a top-down pyramid of power. His wineskin is a family with a heavenly Father who loves us. We are born as His children by the Holy Spirit who is in us. We follow a Brother who is like us in all aspects.

Jesus referred to God as a Father being pleased to give us the kingdom, the harvest being the ingathering of sons, and considered followers to be his brothers. These terms are not meant to be sexist in any way, in the kingdom there is no male and female and all His children are considered 'sons'.

When there is little or no wine (love relationship) present, men instead choose to build complicated, heavy, controlling structures in their own wisdom and after their own image. When the wine is flowing freely it is because the wineskin is patterned according to Father's design; preserving, containing, and pouring out the wine as it was meant to.

For it all to work the Father imparts and exemplifies His own nature and values through His Family; that is the way the wineskin is designed to operate. The simplicity of Father's plan is that in Christ the task is not burdensome but flows freely in the Family of God and brings liberty.

THE AUTHORITY OF CHRIST SEEN IN HOW WE ARE STRUCTURED AS A BODY

Love based relationship is the most important aspect of the kingdom. But it CANNOT establish the kingdom of God by itself. The love relationship we have with both Heavenly Father and our brothers and sisters in the Holy Spirit, has a proper order in which to reside and from which to be poured out. The nature of God is as wine, and the structure that contains and releases it is the wineskin.

The wineskin in its simplest form is people, not an organization, The wineskin that contains the wine of His Love is also described as the many-membered body of Christ. This God ordained structure expresses the love relationship Father desires with all of creation. The structure of the ecclesia is portrayed as a body with different parts and varying operations, functions, and purposes.

"For in the manner that we have many members in one body, nevertheless all the members do not have the same operation; likewise many of us are one body in Christ, and every one members one of another." ~Paul~ (Romans 12:4-5)

Christ is the elder, apostle, prophet, pastor teacher, evangelist, healer, miracle worker, exhorter, encourager, intercessor, and so much more.

He expresses Father's Love through His people as He exercises His authority within each one as He has gifted each one; be it spheres of influence or ministry gifts. These varying operations of Christ's authority through us is how He has 'structured' us uniquely.

This many-membered structure is meant to express the very heart of our Father to creation just as Christ Jesus did to those He was sent to. These gifts of authority, released in and through the body, are truly God Himself expressing His nature through us as He serves and builds up His body. The body, submitting to the Head, works as one in love relationship to express all that Jesus Christ is.

"But speaking the truth in love, we are to grow up in all aspects into Him who is the head, even Christ, from whom the whole body, being fitted and held together by what every joint supplies, according to the proper working of each individual part, causes the growth of the body for the building up of itself in love." ~Paul~ (Ephesians 4:15-16)

CHAPTER EIGHT

'HE COMES'

COMING FOR THE SAKE OF LOVE

As I was speaking to the school Principal about the way my son was being bullied by a bigger boy who kept my son in fear and anxiety during his recess times, I suddenly in anger said, 'If you will not do anything, I will come during break and take care of the problem myself!' The thought of my son, who is slight of build and walks with a prosthetic leg, being tormented again for another year in the school playground evoked a burning anger in me that I could not keep in check.

A previous year of dealing with a problem student who hounded my son each recess trying to kick his private parts and punch him over and over had brought me to the point of saying this year, "No More! If those given responsibility will not protect my son, then I am coming to take care of it myself!"

After my episode with the principle, Father spoke to me and said, "Now, son, you know how I feel about my children!" Father's deep abiding presence came over me.

MAKING SLAVES OF MEN

"I have surely seen the affliction of My people who are in Egypt, and have given heed to their cry because of their taskmasters, for I am aware of their sufferings. So I have come down to deliver them from the power of the Egyptians."
(Exodus 3:7-8 NASB)

I was watching the animated version of the 'Prince of Egypt' soon after this incident, in this movie God spoke to Moses that He had heard the people's cries and had come down to deliver them. I wept like a baby during that movie as the Spirit of God spoke to me and imparted a deep burden of the Lord.

"Now the Egyptian is a man, and not God, and his horses flesh, and not spirit..." (Isaiah 31:3) This verse clearly shows us that Egypt and its horses (strength) represent the flesh of men.

So, let me clearly state that the thing which has enslaved and brought the people of God under fear of men rather than the Fear of the Lord, is LEADERSHIP in the church controlling others with man's fleshly wisdom and works (strength). It has made God's children slaves to men's will and agendas, just as Rameses did thousands of years ago.

THE FEAR OF THE LORD IS COME

The Lord has spoken, *"I will delay no more, I have personally come now to take back what is mine and has been stolen by men, those who have taken My people as captives to their own wills will stand in fear of ME!"*

Father is now coming in power to take back what is His, and those standing in the way will see His displeasure. He is saying to the apostles, prophets and leaders, who like Pharaoh have built their houses on the backs of His Children, "LET MY PEOPLE GO!

I tell you this in all sincerity and without bitterness, God has come down and we are going to see His vengeance for the sake of His sons. Not only has leadership taken advantage of men and instilled the fear of men and doctrines of pleasing and following men in people; many who know better are doing nothing about it.

He comes with the Fear of the Lord in His wake, requiring great repentance and change. There is coming a great diminishing of the positions of men in the church. All of this is simply because it is God putting the church back into HIS righteous order, not the order of hierarchy and title, but the order of Love for God's children. Father is elevating His own Shepherds in this hour, whom He has personally raised up and prepared in secret, 'who will not fleece the sheep, but lay down their lives for them'.

This coming of Jesus Christ within many sons will reveal the divine mysteries and the wisdom of God to all creation. His manifest presence will take preeminence over creation as He sums up all things in Himself. As Adam tried to hide his shame from Father's presence in the garden, so in this day men will try to hide from His coming presence. Yet there will be no place to hide.

Many will scurry like cockroaches seeking dark places when the Light appears. They will cry to the mountains and hills (man's governments and systems) to fall on them and hide them from the face of His glorious presence. Those in hell will not be able to hide from His presence either, as hell's gates will not be able to resist and overcome the light. Demonic forces and those who have become in nature like them, will be in terror and attempt to rally together opposing anyone who bears His name.

The Valley of Decision will be set before all the inhabitants of the earth. Many who believed they knew Him will realize they have in fact opposed His hand and will accept the invitation to repent. Great repentance will sweep His house as the peace of His presence heals and delivers His people into His joy.

Like the coming of Jesus Christ 2000 years ago, there will also be those who resist turning from man's ways and will expend their strength and wisdom to oppose Him. Like the Pharisees, some will believe they are doing good deeds by resisting His coming, yet all they will be doing is undermining and contesting the work of the Spirit on every front. This will only serve to purify the saints, strengthening their resolve and perseverance.

LIVING BY REVELATION OF THE WORD

We do not live by bread alone, but by every continual utterance of Jesus, the Living Word, Himself. Our food is the bread of heaven (Christ) and His quickened words which become Spirit and life to us. We are progressively receiving revelation of Himself through abiding in Him, and we ourselves are BECOMING expressions of His person as we partake of His divine nature.

As Father sent the Son, so the Son (the Word) has sent the sons of Father to walk in the way He walked. We are His sons speaking words of spirit and life to a needy and dying world.

""Abide in Me, and I in you. As the branch cannot bear fruit of itself unless it abides in the vine, so neither can you unless you abide in Me. "I am the vine, you are the branches; he who abides in Me and I in him, he bears much fruit, for apart from Me you can do nothing. "If anyone does not abide in Me, he is thrown away as a branch and dries up; and they gather them, and cast them into the fire and they are burned. "If you abide in Me, and My words abide in you, ask whatever you wish, and it will be done for you. (John 15:4-7 NASB)

As scripture clearly reveals; 'all of creation has groaned and travailed for the revealing of God's mature sons' who are expressions and containers of Christ on the earth today. Christ comes again in His children as the seed He planted 2000 years ago has brought forth fruit after its own kind; sons in the image of their Father. The life-giving Spirit of Jesus Christ abiding in many sons will manifest His tangible presence unto all creation.

Those who partake of the oneness He offers will come to experience the true common-union of the Saints as they have never been known before. They will come to know that the great cloud of witnesses, known as The Church of the First Born in Hebrews 12, is as close to us as our breath is, and that our oneness in Him reaches beyond even the barriers of death. Heaven and its inhabitants in Christ will be partakers of the restoration of creation, even unto resurrection of incorruptible bodies.

In Him our ability to function in and interact with the realms of heaven on earth will cause the veil between the physical and spiritual to lift. The light of His presence will envelope all creation. All things in heaven and on the earth are sustained by Him and shall be fully restored by Him. He will receive His inheritance and shall be the 'all in all'. Rejoice saints of The King, His glorious presence is come to us, is in us and is flowing through us. He will reign forever more.

A FLOOD OF WATER

It is the season of the flood of God's river. The rain is come and the water is rising to lift those in the safety of the Ark as they ascend to the clouds of glory, the flood will satisfy the thirsty soul with life while washing away the filth of lies.

My son, who was ten years old at the time, saw a vision of a fast-moving river that quickly rose up over the heads of the people, it then rose over the buildings (man-made systems) and flowed so that it was even deeper (greater) than our needs. My three-year-old daughter then said that she saw the water wash the mud away from our mouths. My son then saw thousands of people jumping up and down for Joy.

The season of a purifying and life-giving flow from Father is here. This flood will flow greater than our own ability to contain it and bring with it cleansing and a healing flow of life.

LOVE AND JUSTICE

"We have come to know and have believed the love which God has for us. God is love, and the one who abides in love abides in God, and God abides in him." (1 John 4 NASB)

Love is the essence and substance of who our Father is. Throughout history His intention toward creation has been the restoration, redemption, and reconciliation of ALL things to Himself. While the redemptive purposes of God were manifest to men in space and time at the arrival of Jesus Christ; in the mind and heart of God all these were resolved before creation.

Through Jesus Christ, the Father created all things, and in His love, He views creation from beginning to end through the finished work of Jesus Christ, the Lamb slain from before the foundation of the world. He has always been love-incarnate and all His interactions with men, from the beginning of time to its end, flow from His love.

It is Father who defines love; love does not define Him. Holiness, righteousness, goodness, justice, judgment, and even wrath are ALL expressions of His love. Even if they seem to be contradicting each other from our human perspective, they are NOT competing traits in His character!

Apart from knowing Him personally and believing in and receiving His love for us; our finite minds cannot begin to fathom His character, understand the complexities of truth, nor accurately grasp His works and actions toward men and the rest of His creation. The justice of God upon the earth is, and always has been, an expression of God's love both before and after the coming of Christ in the flesh. Both Old and New Testament scriptures clearly declare Father to be a God of Justice, but before everything there is LOVE.

THE JUSTICE OF GOD

Father's purpose in justice is not to delight in the suffering or death of wicked men. His justice comes to deliver us and give relief to mankind from the suffering, oppression, and deception of evil perpetrated by wicked men and devils. Many times, justice comes as the result of the law of sowing and reaping; where God refrains from intervening to rescue wicked men from the consequences of their own evil seeds of wickedness.

It was by love that God allowed all of creation to reap the consequences of the fall that barred the way to the Tree of Life. This was allowed so that the seed of sin might be cut off in death and not continue to propagate suffering endlessly.

It was for HOPE of redemption and freedom from sins corruption that men faced the futility of death. Father did not consider temporal death able to stop His redemptive purposes; but saw that His justice in Christ's victory over death was the hope for freedom from death and restoration of all mankind." (Romans 8:20-21)

But for mercy's sake, He has ordained temporal justice to relieve the suffering of men under the influence of wicked oppressors. The following are some examples from OT scripture that clearly reveal the justice of God, on love's foundation.

Those who died in the flood became corrupt even down to the contamination of their DNA, becoming part human and part fallen-heavenly-beings. Their continual wickedness only caused suffering and oppression for the sons of men. Father brought temporal justice to this corrupted flesh, to ensure His redemptive purpose in Christ would survive through Noah's lineage, and that Jesus' bloodline remained uncorrupted.

This redemptive purpose was fully realized when Jesus descended (I Peter 3:19-20 & Ephesians 4:9-10) and preached to those who had been in Hades, imprisoned within the earth since the days of Noah. Then Jesus led them out of their captivity when He ascended.

The justice of God toward Sodom and Gomorrah was in response to the oppression and suffering that came up as a 'cry' to God, Genesis (18:20-21). Not only was there the cry of a brutalized and abused people; Ezekiel speaks of the iniquity of Sodom as it relates to others, ***"Behold, this was the iniquity of thy sister Sodom: pride, fullness of bread, and abundance of idleness was in her and in her daughters, neither did she strengthen the hand of the afflicted and needy." (Ezekiel 16:49)***

God said of the Israelites in Egypt that He had, 'heard their cry, and had come down to deliver them'. Moses was sent by the Hand of God to deliver the people from Egypt with signs and wonders to judge the 'gods' of Egypt. From His heart of love for man, justice came to relieve the oppressed people.

The Israelites came into the land of Canaan which was populated by tribes of people whose wickedness had reached abominable limits. This promised land was full of giants and corrupt bloodlines no longer fully human. People were subjected to incest, ritualistic abuse and innocent babies were sacrificed by being burned alive to their god, Moloch. It was for the love of the innocent that Father's justice removed this defiling and cruel influence from the land.

NEW COVENANT JUSTICE

Jesus clearly speaks of God's justice by removing all that offends in His kingdom at the end of the age. This once again refers to the fact that where evil oppresses others, the justice of God is released to relieve that oppression.

We are told to rejoice over the retribution of God upon Babylon. Babylon is a city built upon the wisdom and works of men which reigns over the kings of the earth. Babylon is a system of spiritual evil from which men operate 'under its influence'.

The angel said, ***"Rejoice over her, thou heaven, and ye saints, apostles, and prophets; for God has judged your cause upon her.."*** *(Revelation 18:20)*

"...for He has judged the great harlot who was corrupting the earth with her immorality, and he has avenged the blood of his bond-servants on her." (Revelation 19:2 NASB)

Note that when Babylon is judged - heaven rejoices. But also that as we have explored earlier, Babylon is a 'system', or a work of evil. Judgement is not directed at people, but at the fruit of evil wisdom and the works of evil. It is a created structure of wickedness and Paul writes that every man's work will be judged. It is not about punishing people or exacting pain for poor behavior.

There will be pain when every work is revealed, exposed and removed. But that is not the point. Scripture tells us all to 'come out of Babylon', (the wisdom and works of men) so you do not share in its destruction.

Imagine all you have built through the work of your hands was removed and destroyed in a day. This system's fall is bound to affect those entangled with and married to the whore of Babylon. The judgement is not meant to exact pain on men, but to remove worthless mindsets and behaviors.

A joyous Praise Party is recorded in scripture after the justice of God delivers men from the injustice of Babylon as it is exposed and thrown down (Revelation 9:3-7). The justice of God in response to the oppression of evil does not change.

THE DAY OF THE LORD

While many are looking to a literal earthly day in which they consider final judgment comes to the earth, I am convinced that the Day of Judgment is an Age in which ALL creation is restored to Christ. It is truly a 'Day' in the eyes of Father which is an age to mankind. That day is called, 'The Day of the Lord'.

It is a 'great and terrible day' because it will be terrible for many who have built their hopes and dreams upon the wisdom and works of mankind. All that can be shaken will be shaken. It will be great because it will signal the rise of the sons of God. It will be the rise and fall of many.

That Day is now upon us my brothers and sisters. It is the day that Christ fully reveals the Father to men as the full stature (maturity or age) of Christ is manifest and abides in His sons. This age is the day of revealing of things that were hidden or shrouded by man's own perceptions, misinformation, and misguided certainties.

As it relates to Father Himself, a misinformation campaign by the enemy of our souls has depicted Him as He is not. This deep misconception of Father is the seed of errant doctrine and division.

We know that He is love; 'for as He is, so we are in this world'. We know that He desires to bring justice to a world of injustice, for we are the Love and the Justice He is bringing. Justice is come to the world as an expression of the heart and love of God in and among His people, for we are His agents on the earth, announcing and proclaiming the Cross of Christ as the loving justice of Father upon sin and death; that men might live in Him and He in them.

TIMES OF SHAKING

The trouble that is coming upon the earth is the result of the powers of the earth shaking as the kingdom of God comes forth. The dissolution of all things built upon the wisdom and works of men is unavoidable as this age unfolds. The institutions in which men have placed their full confidence will be exposed as no longer being places of refuge and provision.

These troubles will first serve as a purging to the household of Father, as He allows the enemy intent on clinging to power to test and trouble His people. This trouble will serve to wake up and arise to our true identity and destiny as sons and daughters of God. Yet, Father is visiting His house in the midst of trouble with great mercy and justice to bring forth a people who overcome.

Our first priority is not to stop the shaking, but to become a place of refuge and strength for mankind to find peace and rest in the midst of the trouble and shaking.

CHAPTER NINE

THE PLACE OF DIVINE AUTHORITY

FINDING HIS TRUE REST

Our preparation for this unfolding age is to find our place of Rest in Him no matter what circumstances are. Divine Rest in Him is our refuge and provision. Rest is living out fully the promise we are invited to inherit, abiding IN Him and He IN us. We shall be in complete peace and security that is unshaken by every external force or power.

Entering His Hebrews 4 'Rest', releases the wisdom and power of God in our midst which is sufficient to meet the needs of everyone. With this understanding of where our sufficiency comes from, I want to share some aspects of this Rest that we must begin to embrace and manifest that will be an anchor of hope to everyone we touch with the wisdom and power of God in our personal places of influence.

DIVINE WISDOM

"And of the sons of Issachar, two hundred chief men, who had understanding of the times and were wise to know what Israel ought to do; and all their brethren followed their word." *(I Chronicles 12:32)*

In the days of transition from Saul's kingdom to David's kingdom, the sons of Issachar joined David with a particular insight where they 'understood the times and with wisdom knew what to do'. In this current day of transition, as the kingdoms of this world are becoming the kingdoms of our God and of His Christ, we again need to be like the sons of Issachar.

We need Godly counsel, wisdom, understanding and power to know what to do and how to do it. To possess the understanding and wisdom of God is to have the mind of Christ, which is freely available to us.

"For who has known the mind of the lord, that he will instruct him? But we have the mind of Christ.." ~Paul~
(I Corinthians 2:16 NASB)

Before Jesus' death on the cross Peter accepted Jesus, walked on water, had a clear breakthrough revelation of who Jesus was, saw Elijah and Moses on the mountain, healed the sick and cast out devils. Yet, Jesus rebuked him saying, *"But He turned and said to Peter, "Get behind Me, Satan! You are a stumbling block to Me; for you are not setting your mind on God's interests, but man's.". (Matthew 16:23 NASB)* Peter had his own transition to navigate in his day. After being humbled and broken by his abject failure, he received the indwelling Spirit and transitioned from seeing things from the perspective of men to seeing things from the perspective of God and subsequently, even his shadow healed the sick.

Many who claim allegiance to the name of Jesus today are like Peter. We can be born again and be led by the Holy Spirit and still operate with a worldly understanding and wisdom that has the things of men and not God in mind. To have His mind is to think His thoughts and see with His eyes.

THE FAITH OF A CHILD

If the Spirit of God dwells in us we have been given His mind. Yet, our minds must be renewed in conformance to His mind as we are transformed by The Word (Christ) to think and perceive the very thoughts and perceptions of God.

We are transformed by this renewing through childlike faith that lets go of EVERY understanding, preconception, and certainty we have ever held in order to hear and believe Him. This is the faith that leads to Rest.

Today is a day of revelation and understanding that calls for hearts of teachableness and humility. The greatest hindrance to our understanding things from Father's perspective is when we assume that our perspectives are already His.

It took a powerful vision and a voice from heaven given three times from God to convince the Apostle Peter to accept that salvation was meant for the gentiles as well as Jews. Let me tell you that there are many, many things we will need to understand today that we cannot accept because of what religion has taught us, just like Peter in his day. How many times will God need to give us a vision to remove our deeply established certainties on doctrines, theologies, or faith positions before we accept that it is Him?

All our understanding must go through the Cross. Most importantly, the solid doctrines we fear to doubt must be laid as an offering to be done with as He sees fit. When we have abandoned our own accepted understandings, theological wisdom and learned perspectives unto Him, we may just find that we don't think about or see things like we once did, and we will possess His mind just as He possesses our minds.

DIVINE UNITY

"Being diligent to guard the unity of the Spirit in the bond of peace. There is one body and one Spirit, even as ye are called in one hope of your calling, one Lord, one faith, one baptism, one God and Father of all, who is above all and through all, and in you all." (Ephesians 4:3-4)

The body of Christ is 'one body'. This unity of the Spirit found in Jesus Christ cannot be established or extinguished by any leader, institution, doctrine, covenant, or agreement found among men. Men may gather together or separate themselves from others according to these differences, but in Christ there is no division. This unity has already been established in Christ and simply exists; 'all who abide in Him are already one'.

In this hour, those finding their Rest in Christ are discovering a unity with like-minded others by the Holy Spirit that transcends everything that divides men. This divine unity is not going to be trumped by any church or religious affiliation, national allegiance, racial origin, or any other distinction among men.

UNITY OF PURPOSE

Many are being brought into a unity of purpose with people they may not normally associate with in the natural. Preparation for troubled times demands that we are led by the peace of God into relationships and purposes with others that are intended to release the kingdom of God 'on earth as it is in heaven'. Father Himself is making connections 'marked' by a 'bond of peace' as a witness of the true Spirit of God. We must be prepared to join in kingdom purposes with those we hardly know in the flesh, as He leads and guides us.

It is important in this hour to refuse to participate in alliances that are not of the Holy Spirit, regardless of how 'good' the cause or purpose men are promoting. To join in unity of purpose with those with whom we have no Spirit direction or connection will hinder the work and purposes of God in this hour.

We may be 'going to' or be a 'member' of an organized church in our region, while the purpose of God is for us to connect to others who may be spread across our region or many regions.

This book is being published by that same Spirit connection with a man on the other side of the world. He just happened to message me concerning an excerpt of this book I had published on social media. I was just asking Father about who could edit this book, and a man I only knew through social media answered the Spirit without me advertising the need for it. I simply got a message discussing the content of the post, and Father said, "Ask him if he would edit your book." I was grateful to find out he had previous book editing experience.

The kingdom of God is not limited to a 'church' affiliation, nor a local district. It is vital to follow the peace of God's leading to connect with others to extend the eternal purposes for which we have been connected.

DIVINE PROVISION

"And all that believed were together and had all things common and sold their possessions and property and distributed them to everyone, as each one had need." (Acts 2:44-45)

In the early church there was one source of provision for the people of God. Provision to meet daily, family, business and miraculous needs was found in the Divine Unity they shared in common-union. The body of Christ is the expression of Christ and the provision of God to meet the needs of men; first in the household of faith, and then in the world. We are given to each of our neighbors to be their provision, just as every joint supplies the body's needs. As sons of God, we are responsible to produce and provide for others what they are unable to produce for themselves.

Divine Provision is not just limited to physical capital as men see it, but is based upon His heavenly economy, whose currency is Love we give. Physical capital is only one aspect of the provision Father has made available to us in Christ. Whatever the need is, our Father has made provision for it in Christ, and we are His 'hands and feet' to the people of the earth. There are many needs mankind has; healing, friendship, deliverance, understanding, protection, compassion, encouragement, identity, nurturing, correction, physical sustenance, shelter, warmth and clothing etc.

THE ECONOMY OF HEAVEN

It is Father's will for us to not simply be provision to others, but to enable others to walk in provision themselves; so that they, in turn, will become provision for others. For example, we may need healing and Father sends to us one who walks in healing.

While we receive our heavenly healing, we can also receive impartation and understanding to walk in healing power ourselves. This is a true kingdom principle. The kingdom is not one of building networks of dependency upon men, but of Father providing and establishing fullness and sufficiency in every one of His own sons.

While there are situations where direct and prolonged provision is needed for those who cannot meet their own needs, the greatest need many have is to be taught how to produce and provide for others both spiritually and physically.

Paul was clear in writing, *"…if anyone desires not to work neither should he eat." (II Thessalonians 3:10)* But the kingdom of God is also about serving and being a provider for your own needs and for others, not simply producing enough for your own needs or living in a state of dependency upon others.

The reality of Divine provision in Christ that the early apostles walked in was later replaced by worldly men implementing a 10% tax to prop up institutions and leadership structures built by men. This concept was not taught by the apostles but misapplied from Old Testament law. The church tax became the worldly substitute that tragically usurped the means by which Father intended to provide for His children. The restoration of true Divine provision is coming forth in this time and boy do we need it!

"But my God shall supply all your need according to his riches in glory by Christ Jesus." (Philippians 4:19)

The greatest wealth and provision that is available to us from heaven is the love of our Father manifested in Christ Jesus. We are members of His body and partakers of His divine nature. Our preparation for times of shaking is not about looking to men's systems or governments to supply our needs. Our true provision is found in Christ and in Divine Unity with His people. It is important to embrace this unity and be part of the give and take of supply within His body.

DIVINE AUTHORITY

The last aspect of rest I want to share about that Father is releasing to His children is Divine Authority. Everyone who is 'in Christ' has individually been given the power to walk in the fullness of His 'divine authority' in their spheres of both purpose and influence, and also benefits from the divine authority God has placed within others. Jesus did not come to the earth to simply give mankind a 'nice' message of the kingdom.

Nor did he intend that a few 'special ones' go out and do the power stuff while the rest filled the pews waiting for them to return from their ministry trips to great acclaim and the praise of men. He demonstrated the authority of the kingdom by having real heavenly answers for the troubles of men.

Jesus healed the sick, cast out devils, fulfilled OT prophecy, received divine energy through angelic assistance, raised the dead, fed thousands of hungry people, discipled people, commanded turbulent weather to cease, rose from the dead Himself and ascended to the right hand of Father; sending His Spirit in power to help us execute the same authority he had.

There was no situation, trouble, difficulty, or affliction Jesus was incapable of facing because He walked in the authority of heaven. Subsequently, scripture shows us that there was no trouble the first group of apostolic fathers were incapable of facing as they walked in the same authority of heaven. Finally, there is no situation today that we His sons and daughters cannot deal with as we walk in the same authority of heaven!

Jesus said to His disciples, ***"All authority hath been given unto me in heaven and on earth." (Matthew 28:18***) This same Jesus, who has ALL authority then gave it to men. He told the disciples, ***"I give to you the authority to tread upon serpents and scorpions, and on all the power of the enemy, and nothing by any means shall hurt you." (Luke 10:19)***

BINDING AND LOOSING

Jesus told Peter, ***"I will give you the keys of the kingdom of heaven; and whatever you bind (declare to be improper and unlawful) on earth must be what is already bound in heaven; and whatever you loose (declare lawful) on earth must be what is already loosed in heaven." (Mathew 16:19 AMP)***

Jesus has also given US the keys of divine authority to forbid on earth what is already forbidden in heaven and release on earth what is already released in heaven. Everything Jesus did and said originated from heaven; every miracle, healing, teaching and even his death which had already happened in heaven before the foundation of the world (Revelation 13).

He expressed the kingdom of God on the earth, by simply doing what He saw the Father doing in heaven (John 5). The same keys of authority that have been given to you and me, are also intended to release the kingdom of God in the particular places and ways Father has called each of us personally to exercise His Divine authority.

"For I also am a man under authority, having soldiers under me; and I say to this man, Go, and he goes; and to another, Come, and he comes; and to my slave, Do this, and he does it."
~The Centurion~ (Matthew 8:9)

While some want to use the account of the centurion with great faith to inappropriately implement a worldly chain of command in the church, the point of this passage is to show us that great faith is knowing you are fully authorized, under the authority of God Himself, to exercise the divine authority of heaven here on the earth.

Divine authority carries with it all the weight of heaven and flows from the place of Rest that does not struggle to be executed. This authority confidently releases upon earth what is already established and authorized in heaven. If you must work up faith, you do not have the authority. If you have the authority, you simply command it to be, and it is done.

AUTHORITY TO MEET NEEDS

And He said to them, "The kings of the Gentiles lord it over them; and those who have authority over them are called 'Benefactors.' But it is not this way with you, but the one who is the greatest among you must become like the youngest, and the leader like the servant." ~Jesus~ (Matthew 22:25-26 NASB)

Divine authority is not a hierarchal system built upon a chain of command, or dependent upon official titles of authority for its execution. Authority in the kingdom flows freely upon love relationships and not simply because of a titled position.

Where the love of God has waned, titles become predominant, where the love of God flows titles are not predominant and men recognize and receive more easily TRUE divine authority. Those with true divine authority do not need to relate to others based upon a position, but exercise authority to fulfill their call to love and service.

The exercise of Divine authority is to serve the needs of others as provision and intervention for them from Father in whatever their need may be. Jesus is the prime example of one who came to serve the unmet needs of men, exercising divine authority out of His love of mankind.

EVERYTHING WE NEED

"...all things that pertain to life and to godliness are given us of his divine power, through the knowledge of him that has called us by his glory and virtue,..." (2 Peter 1:3)

In Jesus Christ we have available to us everything we need. He is our divine wisdom, unity, provision and authority, and He is sufficient for all things and in all times of trouble and need. Our preparation is to walk as sons in His rest that releases in us and through us the divine realities of His being.

This is the kingdom of God; Christ in us manifesting His will and kingdom 'on earth as it is in heaven'. To prepare for the coming times of shaking, we need His discernment to walk hearing and heeding the Spirit of God as to our own divine authority, not substituting positions or titles among men for true divine authority.

We must also recognize and receive the divine authority that rests upon others. When we receive His divine authority manifest in the lives of others, we truly receive Him. As we personally and in unity execute and express divine authority upon the earth, we are manifesting Him and His kingdom to men; which is what is truly needed in both peaceful and troubled times.

THE SPIRIT BEHIND THE DEVOURER

On Tuesday, June 26th, 2012, high temperatures and winds gusting up to 65 mph caused a forest fire to overcome a fire line set up by brave men and women to protect the city of Colorado Springs. The city began to burn, and 36,000 people were evacuated along with the Air Force Academy located nearby.

I saw the images of the city burning on television and decreed a prayer of protection over the people. Then, that night I had a dream. In the dream a wolf was advancing toward me. My dog was trying to fight off the wolf but was overcome by the wolf. When the wolf got past my dog and approached me, I saw the face of an evil spirit behind it.

The Holy Spirit spoke to me, ***"Son, you must separate the spirit behind the devourer from the devourer."***

I looked at the wolf and said to the spirit empowering it, "I cut you off". The glowing fiery-red face of the spirit in the wolf disappeared and the wolf's face went back to its usual dark visage. The wolf then turned and ran away.

The next day the tide turned in the fight against the fire as the temperature began to subside and rain began to fall. On the day after, the temperature dropped further, and the winds died down and the city was spared. An official stated it was the first day that the weather had cooperated since the fire had begun.

AUTHORITY IN REST

Is it possible to simply decree something and it is done? Some would call my dream and declaration and the change of weather a coincidence. Whether it was a coincidence or not, this dream came during the time Father began speaking to me about walking in the authority of 'oneness' with Him. He called me to commune with Him 'within me' as His resting place, and to abide in Him in the place He has seated me in Christ, in the heavenly places.

This truth of resting in Him as He rests in me, has given me a completely new perspective that sees how differently the authority and rule of heaven is executed upon the earth than I was taught in the church paradigm. It is the 'oneness with Him and His heart' that enables us to decree a thing and it is done, for it is Christ that lives in me and in me that speaks and it is done.

Since that time, the Spirit has continued to renew my mind concerning how the will of God is accomplished upon the earth. I have been confronted with multiple situations since then in which Father has not told me what to say but has asked me to make a judgment and speak with His authority as a son, trusting His heart in me as to what to decree into each situation.

Jesus simply spoke to the wind and waves, *"Be Still!"* and it was done. Jesus did not beg Father to answer a prayer; He spoke the will of Father into the situations on earth from His place of Peace and Rest that did not question whether it would be done. He knew He was 'one with Father' and was doing what Father was doing.

I heard a testimony where a group of fearful missionaries asked God to protect them from a huge storm that was about to hit. "No", said Father "I won't stop the storm." Perplexed, they cried out, "Why not? Don't You love us?" Father then spoke, "My dear children, of course I love you, but my son showed you how to deal with a storm – so you do it!"

Ruling over the circumstances of life proceeds out of the place of rest where we know we are one with Him and are seated in Him. If He moves us to speak to it, then He has given His heart and authority to execute the will of heaven in the situation and it is done!

A PLACE TO RULE

I am convinced the dream I shared is for the sake of encouraging myself and others to seek further to find the place of rule in the kingdom that Father has prepared for each of us.

- He is transitioning us from a slave and begging mentality to receiving our full and complete inheritance and identity as sons and daughters of the King.
- He is teaching us to trust His heart and judgments within us as we face circumstances and overcome them with His goodness.
- He is showing us that by Him dwelling in us and our Resting in places of authority in Him, where He has seated us, 'we can do ALL things through Christ who strengthens us'.
- He is teaching us to speak forth the decrees of heaven into situations from a heart that already knows His will, rather than us beseeching Father to know whether we should do what He already commissioned and enabled us to do.

Christ in me is sufficient for all things and He is 'no respecter of persons', so we have access to the same authority and power and abilities that Jesus revealed during His three years of ministry.

I have come to believe that Father is not looking for men and women to beg Him to move His hand; He is looking for men and women of courage and might to BE His hands and feet upon the earth.

He is not looking for those who cry out from earth to bring heaven down; He is looking for those who KNOW that they ARE seated in the heavens with Him to manifest His preeminence and will in the earth.

This IS the kingdom of God come to earth. If you know you are seated in Him and He is at Rest in you, then you can speak what He is saying and what you decree is done, just as Jesus did.

Therefore, if you have been raised with Christ, keep seeking the things that are above, where Christ is, seated at the right hand of God. Set your minds on the things that are above, not on the things that are on earth. For you have died, and your life is hidden with Christ in God. When Christ, who is our life, is revealed, then you also will be revealed with Him in glory.

(Colossians 3:1-4 NASB)